Jedrzej Rybicki

Cooperative Traffic Information Systems

Jedrzej Rybicki

Cooperative Traffic Information Systems

Based on Peer-to-Peer Networks

Südwestdeutscher Verlag für Hochschulschriften

Impressum/Imprint (nur für Deutschland/only for Germany)
Bibliografische Information der Deutschen Nationalbibliothek: Die Deutsche Nationalbibliothek verzeichnet diese Publikation in der Deutschen Nationalbibliografie; detaillierte bibliografische Daten sind im Internet über http://dnb.d-nb.de abrufbar.
Alle in diesem Buch genannten Marken und Produktnamen unterliegen warenzeichen-, marken- oder patentrechtlichem Schutz bzw. sind Warenzeichen oder eingetragene Warenzeichen der jeweiligen Inhaber. Die Wiedergabe von Marken, Produktnamen, Gebrauchsnamen, Handelsnamen, Warenbezeichnungen u.s.w. in diesem Werk berechtigt auch ohne besondere Kennzeichnung nicht zu der Annahme, dass solche Namen im Sinne der Warenzeichen- und Markenschutzgesetzgebung als frei zu betrachten wären und daher von jedermann benutzt werden dürften.

Verlag: Südwestdeutscher Verlag für Hochschulschriften GmbH & Co. KG
Dudweiler Landstr. 99, 66123 Saarbrücken, Deutschland
Telefon +49 681 37 20 271-1, Telefax +49 681 37 20 271-0
Email: info@svh-verlag.de

Approved by: Düsseldorf, HHU, Diss., 2011

Herstellung in Deutschland:
Schaltungsdienst Lange o.H.G., Berlin
Books on Demand GmbH, Norderstedt
Reha GmbH, Saarbrücken
Amazon Distribution GmbH, Leipzig
ISBN: 978-3-8381-2941-9

Imprint (only for USA, GB)
Bibliographic information published by the Deutsche Nationalbibliothek: The Deutsche Nationalbibliothek lists this publication in the Deutsche Nationalbibliografie; detailed bibliographic data are available in the Internet at http://dnb.d-nb.de.
Any brand names and product names mentioned in this book are subject to trademark, brand or patent protection and are trademarks or registered trademarks of their respective holders. The use of brand names, product names, common names, trade names, product descriptions etc. even without a particular marking in this works is in no way to be construed to mean that such names may be regarded as unrestricted in respect of trademark and brand protection legislation and could thus be used by anyone.

Publisher: Südwestdeutscher Verlag für Hochschulschriften GmbH & Co. KG
Dudweiler Landstr. 99, 66123 Saarbrücken, Germany
Phone +49 681 37 20 271-1, Fax +49 681 37 20 271-0
Email: info@svh-verlag.de

Printed in the U.S.A.
Printed in the U.K. by (see last page)
ISBN: 978-3-8381-2941-9

Copyright © 2011 by the author and Südwestdeutscher Verlag für Hochschulschriften GmbH & Co. KG and licensors
All rights reserved. Saarbrücken 2011

Abstract

This thesis deals with cooperative traffic information systems, which support the driver of a car in selecting a route, based on traffic information collected by other cars. System participants contribute measurements of the traffic situation in their vicinity (e. g., current traffic flow speed) and use the measurements made by other drivers to find the fastest route to their destination with regard to the current conditions. Such systems help avoid traffic jams, highly congested roads, place of accidents and other unexpected deterioration.

The communication pattern of the discussed application is quite challenging: continuously updated data (i. e., description of the current traffic conditions) are to be made available to multiple participants spread over relatively large geographical areas. Cooperative traffic information systems have primarily been discussed in the context of direct, ad-hoc communication between cars. We formally show in this thesis that a very special communication properties of the discussed application do not fit into the constrained capacity offered by mobile ad-hoc networks. Consequently, this work proposes an alternative design, based on a peer-to-peer paradigm and cellular networks, to efficiently distribute traffic information.

Since the data maintained in a cooperative traffic information system have a very specific structure, it is particularly profitable—in terms of bandwidth consumption and latency—to tailor the system to this specific application domain instead of re-using generic peer-to-peer approaches. In our work we shall point out the limitations of generic P2P networks when it comes to the exchange of dynamic traffic related data. Then we will present Peer-to-Peer-based cooperative Traffic Information System: *PeerTIS*. That is an adjusted generic peer-to-peer overlay, which accounts for the special properties of the discussed application. In addition to a detailed description of such adjustments, we will also provide evaluation showing the technical feasibility of the peer-to-peer-based traffic information system.

Although PeerTIS is a step forward towards an efficient implementation of a working inter-vehicular application, it still possesses some limitations. In particular, the unfair load distribution among the participants of PeerTIS might undermine the idea of cooperative systems, with all the participants being equal in rights and obligations. Thus latter in the thesis we will take a significant step further and develop *GraphTIS*—a peer-to-peer network specifically designed to manage traffic information. It is a novel peer-to-peer system that has specifically been designed to support traffic information systems. It preserves the structure of the stored data, allowing for a quick and efficient retrieval of the data, at the same time avoiding the pitfalls of PeerTIS.

The efficient retrieval of the data stored in a traffic information system is only the first part of the complete solution. The data stored in the system are dynamic, thus a mechanism for keeping in touch with the updates must also be developed and implemented. In this thesis we will present a novel approach to achieve this aim. We will extend our peer-to-peer system with a publish/subscribe module to distribute the updates efficiently.

The efficiency and feasibility of our algorithms are important properties of the proposed solution, but even more important is the assessment of the potential benefit for the user which our system can offer when deployed. We will devote a separate chapter of the work to the problem of dynamic routing with availability of traffic information. We discuss two possible routing algorithms and compare them in a simulation environment composed of a network simulator and the fully-fledged car traffic simulator SUMO. By using a traffic simulator and maps of a real agglomeration we increase the plausibility of the evaluation. Our results show that when deployed, the system can indeed bring benefits to its users by reducing the average travel times of the simulated cars.

Acknowledgments

First and foremost I want to express my gratitude to the people who supported me, as a person, during my work. This thesis is dedicated to my family, in particular to my mother Maria, my wonderful wife Magda and the best sister I have ever had: Marianna.

I am also very thankful to my doctoral advisers, Martin Mauve and Björn Scheuermann. This two excellent teachers have kept inspiring me over the years and allowed me to follow my aspirations.

I appreciate the very friendly, relaxed yet inspiring atmosphere created by my colleagues from the Computer Networks and Communication Systems group in Düsseldorf. It is hard to overestimate their contribution. One person though, Michael Stini, deserved a special thanks, he was always very helpful and made my first years in Germany much easier.

Last but not least I thank people who invested their time helping me in accomplishing less-pleasant but necessary task accompanying the process of writing the thesis. Daniel, Pascal, Frederik, Markus, Norbert, Konstantin, Christian and Marcin helped me by either debugging the code, providing manuscript reviews or solving other technical problems.

Contents

List of Figures   ix

List of Tables   xi

List of Abbreviations   xiii

1 Introduction   1

2 Traffic Information Systems   7
     2.1 Motivation 7
     2.2 Possible implementations 8
         2.2.1 Stationary traffic sensors 9
         2.2.2 Cellular floating phone data 11
         2.2.3 Floating car data 12
         2.2.4 Cooperative traffic information systems 12
     2.3 Measurements 18
     2.4 Communication paradigms 19
     2.5 System specification 21

3 Vehicular Ad-Hoc Networks   23
     3.1 Research projects on inter-vehicular communication 24
     3.2 Applications overview 27
         3.2.1 Road safety applications 28
         3.2.2 Traffic efficiency applications 31
         3.2.3 Value-added applications 32
     3.3 VANET limitations 34
         3.3.1 Limited connectivity 34
         3.3.2 Limited capacity 37
     3.4 Conclusion 53

4 UMTS and Peer-to-Peer   55
     4.1 Universal Mobile Telecommunications System (UMTS) 56
     4.2 Peer-to-Peer 61
     4.3 Conclusion 70

5 A Peer-to-Peer Structure for Traffic Information Systems — 73
- 5.1 The TIS application 74
  - 5.1.1 Framework and use case 74
  - 5.1.2 Tackling a TIS with P2P techniques 75
- 5.2 A P2P overlay for traffic information systems 76
  - 5.2.1 Naive approach 77
  - 5.2.2 Improving the look-up performance 78
  - 5.2.3 Load distribution 81
  - 5.2.4 Exploiting temporal correlations 83
- 5.3 Evaluation 84
  - 5.3.1 Simulation setup 84
  - 5.3.2 Feasibility 86
  - 5.3.3 Performance 90
- 5.4 Conclusion 92

6 Graph-based Peer-to-Peer Structure — 95
- 6.1 A street graph-based approach 95
- 6.2 Distributing a structured key space 97
  - 6.2.1 Key neighbor graphs 100
  - 6.2.2 Partitioning the key neighbor graph 101
  - 6.2.3 Graph partitioning algorithms 103
- 6.3 Protocol 105
  - 6.3.1 Assumptions and overview 105
  - 6.3.2 Locating a single, arbitrary key 108
  - 6.3.3 Requesting a set of correlated keys 110
  - 6.3.4 Improving the look-up complexity 110
  - 6.3.5 Overlay maintenance: join, leave, and recovery 114
  - 6.3.6 Look-up complexity 116
- 6.4 Evaluation 117
  - 6.4.1 Simulation setup 118
  - 6.4.2 Comparison with generic DHTs 118
  - 6.4.3 Choosing the partitioning algorithm 121
  - 6.4.4 External edge weights 123
  - 6.4.5 Improvements of the initial look-up 125
  - 6.4.6 Scalability 128
  - 6.4.7 Comparison with PeerTIS 128
- 6.5 Conclusion 131

7 Application Evaluation — 133
- 7.1 Related work 134
  - 7.1.1 User benefits in cooperative traffic information systems .. 134
  - 7.1.2 Decision making 137

	7.2	Publish/Subscribe	139
	7.3	Dynamic vehicle routing	141
		7.3.1 Initial routing decision	141
		7.3.2 Keeping in touch with the development of the situation	142
	7.4	Evaluation	143
		7.4.1 Simulation setup	143
		7.4.2 Dynamic routing	144
		7.4.3 Publish/Subscribe	148
	7.5	Conclusion	150

8 Conclusions   **153**

A Lemma Proofs   **161**
   A.1 Proof of Lemma 3.1 161
   A.2 Proof of Lemma 3.2 162
   A.3 Proof of Lemma 3.3 162

B Range Queries   **165**

Bibliography   **171**

Index   **184**

List of Figures

2.1	Overview of a traffic information system.	8
3.1	The total communication bandwidth into a circle of finite radius.	43
3.2	Primary and secondary circles in the construction of M^*.	49
4.1	The architecture of the UMTS network.	56
4.2	Distribution of data among peers in a Chord overlay network.	67
5.1	Naive application of CAN to a TIS.	79
5.2	Preservation of the road network structure in the PeerTIS overlay.	81
5.3	Average peer bandwidth usage.	87
5.4	Scalability: Average peer bandwidth usage.	87
5.5	Per-cell network usage in 5 s time slots.	89
5.6	Load distribution in the network.	89
5.7	Bandwidth usage history of the busiest peers.	90
5.8	Total number of hops needed to query a complete route.	91
5.9	Effects of contact caching in PeerTIS.	92
6.1	Sequence of joins in one region of overlay in PeerTIS.	96
6.2	Distribution of the query sizes in PeerTIS.	98
6.3	A fragment of a street map and the corresponding key neighbor graph.	99
6.4	Map of Düsseldorf partitioned with KL-GM algorithm.	104
6.5	Partitioning tree of a graph.	106
6.6	Additional edge in a lattice.	111
6.7	Asymptotic number of hops needed to retrieve information on 100 segments length route.	117
6.8	Total number of hops needed to query a complete route.	119
6.9	Average number of unique peers contacted per queried segment.	120
6.10	Total number of hops needed to query a complete route (zoomed).	121
6.11	Node degree distribution.	122
6.12	Effects of external edge weights (KL-GM).	123
6.13	Effects of external edge weights (KL-BFS).	124
6.14	Effects of additional connections.	125
6.15	Effects of peer contact caching and Geojoins.	126

6.16 Effects of simultaneous peer contact caching and Geojoins. 127
6.17 Scalability: Average peer bandwidth usage. 128
6.18 Total number of hops needed to query a complete route: differences between PeerTIS and GraphTIS. 129
6.19 Average bandwidth usage in the network. 130
6.20 Load distribution in the network. 131

7.1 Travel times improvement (Greedy). 145
7.2 Travel times improvement (AltRoute). 146
7.3 Comparison of travel times improvement. 146
7.4 Total bandwidth usage caused by the application. 148
7.5 Publish/Subscribe: Travel time improvements (Greedy). 149
7.6 Publish/Subscribe: Travel time improvements (AltRoute). 149
7.7 Publish/Subscribe: Bandwidth usage (Greedy). 150
7.8 Publish/Subscribe: Bandwidth usage (AltRoute). 151

B.1 Bounding box containing a planned journey (Route 66 from Chicago to Los Angeles). 168

List of Tables

3.1 Important Inter-Vehicular Communication Projects. 27

List of Abbreviations

3GPP	3rd Generation Partnership Project
AES	Advanced Encryption Standard
BFS	Breadth-first search
C2CCC	Car-2-Car Communication Consortium
CAN	Content Addressable Network
CCW	Cooperative Collision Warning System
CDF	Cumulative Distribution Function
CFPD	Cellular Floating Phone Data
CN	UMTS Core Network Subset
DACH	UMTS Dedicated Channel
DHT	Distributed Hash Table
DNS	Domain Name System
DOT	U. S. Department of Transportation
DSL	Digital Subscriber Line
DSRC	Dedicated Short Range Communication Standard
DTN	Delay Tolerant Network
ECL	Event Code List
EIR	UMTS Equipment Identify Register
FACH	UMTS Forward Access Channel
FCC	Federal Communication Commission
FCD	Floating Car Data
FTAP	Fast Traffic Alert Protocol

GGSN	GPRS Support Node
GM	Geometric Partitioning
GPS	Global Positioning System
HLR	UMTS Home Location Register
IP	Internet Protocol
ISO	International Standards Organization
ISO OSI	ISO Open Systems Interconnection model
ITS	Intelligent Transportation System
IVC	Inter Vehicular Communication
KL-GM	Kernighan-Lin Geometric Partitioning
LAI	UMTS Location Area Index
LAN	Local Area Network
LCL	Location Code List
LTE	3GPP Long Term Evolution Network
MAAN	Multi-Addressable Network
MBMS	UMTS Multimedia Broadcast Multicast Service
MD5	Message-Digest Algorithm 5
MIMO	Multiple-Input Multiple-Output Antennas
MSC	UMTS Mobile Switching Center
P2P	Peer-to-peer
PDP	Packet Data Protocol
RACH	UMTS Random Access Channel
RNC	UMTS Radio Network Controller
RNS	UMTS Radio Network Subsystem
RSU	Road Side Units
SFC	Space Filling Curve
SGSN	Serving GPRS Support Node
SOTIS	Self Organizing Traffic Information System

TIS	Traffic Information System
TTL	Time-to-Live
UE	UMTS User Equipment
UMTS	Universal Mobile Telecommunications System
UTC	Coordinated Universal Time
UTRA	UMTS Terrestrial Radio Access Network
UTRA-FDD	UTRA Frequency Division Duplex
UTRA-TDD	UTRA Time Division Duplex
VANET	Vehicular Ad-Hoc Network
VLR	UMTS Visitor Location Register
VRP	Vehicle Routing Problem
WLAN	Wireless Local Area Network

Chapter 1

Introduction

Within the short period of time since their invention, cars have become a very important part of our everyday life. Their presence is so commonplace that we forget how often we rely on their service. They bring us to work, to our families and are widely used as a means of public transportation and for transporting goods. According to the statistics published by the European Automobile Manufacturers Association (ACEA) [Ace], in 2008 fleet volume, that is the number of vehicles in use, in the EU comprised of about 234 million units, 134 in the USA and over 57 million in Japan. Car density, that is the number of registered cars per 1000 inhabitants, was 470 in the EU, 450 in Japan and 444 in the USA. Despite the economic meltdown of the recent years, the number of new passenger cars registered in 2009 amounted to over 1 million units in Europe. As the cars are part of our lives, so are their dark sides: air pollution, car accidents, traffic congestion, etc. It can be expected that the problems will intensify, especially in city environments. According to the Global Report on Human Settlements [Setb] prepared by the United Nations Center for Human Settlements (Habitat), the level of urbanization (that is the percentage of population in urban settlements) changed from 67 % to 75 % in Europe in the recent 20 years, and will further increase to 83 % in the year 2025. Efficient transportation in city environments will apparently remain a challenge for a longer period of time.

It is hard to expect that the number of cars on the roads will suddenly go down. The number of cars will rather increase, particularly in city areas due to the increasing urbanization. The capacity of the road network, on the other hand, is clearly upper-bounded. Thus a challenge arises in determining how to use the limited resources more efficiently so as to make traveling by car safer, enjoyable and more efficient. This thesis will present a possible solution to relieve the problem of congestion, a type of *Intelligent Transportation Systems* called Traffic Information Systems (TIS). Such systems provide the drivers with a detailed picture of the current traffic situation in a given area and enable dynamic navigation. They can be viewed as a natural evolution of the currently widely available on-board navigation systems. Current systems use static maps to determine the shortest path to the planned destination. Due to congestion and other unexpected incidents this shortest path is not always the fastest one. Traffic information systems, on the other hand, allow navigation units to use *dynamic up-to-date* maps for the calculations. As a result, they avoid traffic jams, make optimal routing decisions and guide the drivers to their destinations along the fastest routes.

Since traffic congestion also has an economic dimension a lot of effort has been invested among car manufacturers, governments and the academia in the search for better solutions. Consequently the problem of exchanging data in a vehicular environment has been addressed by many research projects such as FleetNet, C2CC, or sim^{TD} [Enk03, C2C, sim]. They have mainly focused on the development of so-called *Vehicular Ad-Hoc Networks* (VANETs) in which cars communicate directly with Wi-Fi-like equipment and form a communication network in an ad-hoc fashion each time it is needed. This principle works fine for a small group of cars in a limited geographical area. However, as we will formally show later in this thesis, when it comes to communication over longer distances and involving many cars, VANET inherently suffers from bad connectivity and constrained capacity. Last but not least, VANETs are not yet available and thus cannot alleviate in the near future the urgent problem of high congestion.

Undeniably, traffic information systems and dynamic navigation are very desirable applications, and so alternative ways should be examined of implementing them. It is specifically solutions which can be applied right *now* that are sought after. Our work has identified the underlying network (VANET) as a limiting factor as far as inter-vehicular applications are concerned. Therefore in this thesis we will present a novel, alternative approach to the implementation of such applications. In particular, infrastructure cellular networks, such as UMTS or GSM, will be leveraged to build working traffic information systems. At the same time, we will follow the idea of cooperative effort of system participants for collecting the data. That is, each participant can share its observation about the traffic conditions in its vicinity, which is then made available to all users. Cooperative collection of the data results in a system where a large number of participants act as mobile traffic sensors. Thus a detailed view of the traffic situation can be obtained, which is qualitatively better than in systems using only static traffic sensors. In order to achieve good scalability, fault tolerance and in order to reflect the cooperative character of the application, we will employ a peer-to-peer paradigm for efficient exchange of the data between cars.

The main contributions of this thesis are as follows:

1. identification of special properties and characteristics of traffic information systems,

2. formal description of the limitations of VANET for the exchange of traffic related information,

3. design of peer-to-peer structures adjusted for special properties of the traffic information system,

4. application of a peer-to-peer-based publish/subscribe system for an efficient distribution of notifications about the observed changes in traffic conditions,

5. feasibility study of our solutions,

6. assessments of potential user gains of the working system.

Structure

The remainder of this thesis is structured as follows.

We start off with a description of general system design of a cooperative traffic information system as we consider it—for the sake of clarity and in order to establish a common terminology. Chapter 2 comprises the architecture and design details of a traffic information system and presents the special properties of the application based on a review of related work on this subject. We will discuss the possible sources of traffic measurements, paradigms and communication networks which can be employed for data exchange.

Chapter 3 presents the state of the art of the IVC research, typical applications envisioned for car-to-car communication and provides detailed insights into technical problems connected with Vehicular Ad-Hoc Networks. Furthermore, we present a framework for a formal study and assessment of the limitations of VANET with special regard to traffic information systems.

Since this thesis will follow an alternative way of implementing traffic information systems based on infrastructure cellular networks, in Chapter 4 we provide the reader with the fundamentals of the UMTS, as an example of an infrastructure cellular network. This part of the thesis will also present knowledge about peer-to-peer overlays that is necessary to follow our further argumentation.

Chapter 5 includes a baseline implementation of the peer-to-peer based traffic information system. Especially we underpin the benefits of preserving the geographical proximity of the data stored in such system. We shall not only show that inter-vehicular communication possess some special properties with regard to query pattern and structure of the stored data that should be accounted for by the underlying peer-to-peer structure, but also assess the potential benefits of such adjustments in a realistic simulation study.

In Chapter 6 we go a significant step further, and show a peer-to-peer structure designed with a concrete application (TIS) in mind. The design aims at preserving the structure of the data stored in the system in a more holistic and general way. We will compare the new peer-to-peer overlay with our previous solution to emphasize the differences.

Chapter 7 assesses the potential gains (that is travel time improvements) that the participants of our system can expect. We use a full-fledged traffic simulator and real street maps to make the evaluation realistic. We also present different dynamic routing strategies that can be employed to derive optimal car routes when the traffic information system is in place. The data stored in the system are dynamic, thus a mechanism for keeping in touch with the updates must also be developed and implemented. In this chapter we will present a novel approach to achieve this aim. We will extend our peer-to-peer system with a publish/subscribe module to distribute the updates efficiently.

Finally, conclusions are presented in Chapter 8.

Chapter 2

Traffic Information Systems

This thesis presents a novel approach to implementing traffic information systems. The idea of TIS is however not new. Therefore in this chapter we will first define what we understand under the term of traffic information system, and then discuss other works on this subject and systematize their contribution. We conclude the chapter with a specification of communication requirements of the traffic information system application.

2.1 Motivation

Due to the rapid increase in the number of cars driving on the roads, the road network has been pushed to its limits, leading to congestion, and waste of time and money. The U.S. Department of Transportation in its report from 2005 [dot05] defines congestion as:

Definition (Congestion). *Congestion is an excess of vehicles on a portion of roadway at a particular time resulting in speeds that are slower, sometimes much slower, than normal or "free flow" speeds. Congestion often means stopped or stop-and-go traffic.*

According to the report the main causes of congestion are: bottlenecks and limited road network capacity (40%), traffic accidents (25%), work zones and

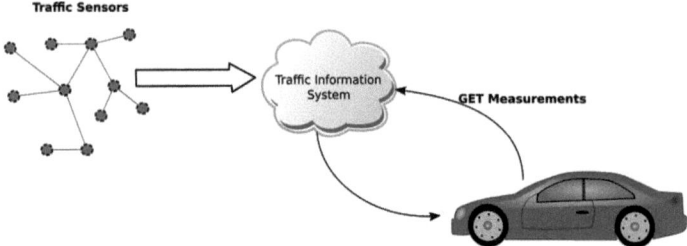

Figure 2.1: Overview of a traffic information system.

constructional activities (25 %) and bad weather (15 %). It is estimated that in the USA congestion caused 3.7 billion hours of travel delay and 8.7 billion liters of wasted fuel, the total cost reaching 63 billion dollars for the year 2005 [dot05]. It is thus not surprising that solutions are sought to increase traffic efficiency and reduce congestion. One possible way to relieve the congestion is to employ intelligent transportation systems and inter-vehicular communication to make more efficiently use of the available resources, in particular to inform drivers about the bottlenecks, traffic accidents and constructional activities.

2.2 Possible implementations

In this thesis we will focus on traffic efficiency applications that can be subsumed under the term *traffic information systems (TIS)*. Traffic information systems are systems providing users with information about the current traffic status, thus enabling so-called dynamic navigation. Figure 2.1 presents a simplified overview of a traffic information system. It is comprised of sensors for collecting traffic measurements, a mechanism for storing and accessing the measurements, system participants and a communication channel to access the data.

In this work we will focus on the case of the distribution of descriptions of current, up-to-date traffic conditions. It has been shown (e. g., [PBB+08]) that such systems potentially offer more benefits than systems using historical floating car data. The working assumption of the latter ones is that there exists a correlation between traffic conditions recorded in the past and a future development: knowing the current situation and historical data, it is then possible to estimate the traveling times in the future. The assumption holds unless something unexpected happens, e. g., an accident, construction work or a social event. The works of Yang et al. [YLSW10] have shown that the routes calculated with historical data are better than those calculated when no data were available at all about the traffic conditions; however, the routes calculated using real-time data are still superior. The authors also demonstrate in their experiments cases in which historical information about travel speed differs widely from real-time data. This motivates the use of a real-time traffic information system and requires the presence of a communication network.

2.2.1 Stationary traffic sensors

The first prerequisite to make a traffic information system work is the availability of measurements of the current traffic situation. These can be obtained in various ways. The first possibility is to deploy a network of stationary traffic sensor units (such as inductive loops [Rot09], infrared sensors or video cameras [Ruh]) to conduct the measurements. Coifman has demonstrated that the most popular traffic sensors used today (the inductive loops) yield noisy and generally inaccurate velocity measurements [Coi99], thus limiting their applicability for gaining real time traffic measurements. Therefore, existing intelligent transportation systems usually use more sophisticated traffic sensors. For instance, the designers of the RuhrPilot project [Ruh] have decided to use over 1 000 autonomous detectors placed along the highways in the largest urban agglomeration in Europe (German *Ruhrgebiet*). The traffic detector used most widely in this project is the *Traffic Eye* device produced by Siemens Mobility Solutions [Sie]. Such a detector is a self-sustaining system with its own power supply provided by solar panels, a communication channel (GSM) and, of course, detectors. The detection of the current traffic status is performed by a passive infrared measurement of the speed and length of passing cars. From such simple measurements other metrics can be derived of the current traffic conditions: average traffic flow speed, occupancy level of the monitored street, etc.. Similarly, TomTom HD Traffic [Tom] and TMC [tmc] use data from various sensors placed along the roads.

Nevertheless, covering large areas with a network of static traffic sensors might become prohibitively expensive. It works quite well on highways where the car flow remains unchanged between consecutive exits (as there are no cars joining or leaving the traffic). In such cases it is possible to conduct the measurements only in the vicinity of the highway exits and extrapolate the results to the remaining part of the highway. Such an approach, however, will not work well in city scenarios, where the traffic flow is less predictable. A large number of sensors would have to be deployed in order to capture the fact that a car can leave or join the traffic at each street junction or even between the junctions.

A high density of sensors will be hard to bring together with the addressing scheme widely used in contemporary navigation units. Most of them rely on the Location Code List (LCL) and Event Code List (ECL) standards used in TMC. Only for locations listed in LCL is it possible to exchange dynamic information in the form of ECL codes. The list is defined by a government organization for each country separately. For instance in Germany it is a prerogative of the Federal Ministry of Transport, Building and Urban Development (BMVBS). The list is relatively short, as it encompasses only about 40 000 distinct locations [lcl], most of them part of the highway system.

The level of detail provided by stationary sensors is also proportional to the sampling frequency which is usually kept low in order to reduce the communication costs of the server and sensor [LSL$^+$08]. And again there is a difference in the dynamics of traffic flow changes between the highway and city scenarios. In the latter case traffic jams can arise much faster [CSS00]. Clearly, increasing the rate the data are to be captured increases the amount of the data that need to be collected and (usually centrally) processed.

2.2.2 Cellular floating phone data

An alternative way of obtaining traffic measurements involves the use of mobile sensors. TomTom HD Traffic [Tom] mentioned above is actually a hybrid solution. Not only data from road sensors are incorporated into the TIS but also anonymous information is used from the GSM network operator on the number of participating phones in GSM cells along main roads. The data are used to guesstimate the current traffic conditions in a given area. This approach is called Cellular Floating Phone Data (CFPD). The cellular network "knows" where the participants are located (which antennas they are currently registered with). When a large concentration of network users is observed in a particular cell, a conclusion can be drawn regarding suboptimal traffic conditions in this area. The system was originally tested on highways around Stockholm and it is not clear if such an approach provides a satisfactory level of detail in city scenarios, where the number of streets in one GSM or UMTS cell is higher, making it hard to attribute the increased density of users in a cell to a particular road and lane. Additionally, there are also other means of public transportation with multiple cell phone carriers on board, rendering the recognition of traffic jams less accurate. The authors have acknowledged the fact [Tom05], and suggested that use of additional traffic sensors can mitigate the problem. As we have already argued, the use of traffic sensors in city scenarios significantly increases the costs of the system.

It should be noticed that only the movement of a fraction of traffic participants will be captured by the system in any case. The reason for that is the need for a tight cooperation between the traffic system operator (TomTom in this case) and the cellular network operator (Vodafone). The latter party has to make data available about the internal network state for external analysis. Clearly only cellular phones using a particular network will produce input for the system. The same holds for receiving the information: only Vodafone users which pay TomTom a fee can access the data.

2.2.3 Floating car data

The idea of using mobile traffic sensors (like cell phones) instead of static ones is quite interesting and constitutes the basis for many further systems. Instead of guesstimating the situation on a given road by analyzing the movement of cell phones it is also possible to retrieve traffic measurements in a more direct manner. Moving cars equipped with GPS can simply inform the system about their position and speed. A solution presented in [STBW02] uses floating car data generated by hundreds of vehicles of taxi companies in Berlin, Nuremberg and Vienna. The data are collected, transmitted to a central server, analyzed and sent back to the participants. An interesting fact regarding this system is that the cars only send their (anonymous) GPS positions periodically. These are then mapped onto street segments and travel times are derived from multiple measurements.

Another system using floating car data is PITA [Rot09]. Real-time measurements are collected only by taxis and some delivery trucks. The vehicles send their position and status periodically with a sampling rate of about once every minute. The measurements are aggregated and analyzed on the server and made available to the participants.

In both systems, the expected level of detail is upper-bounded due to the fact that the measurements are only conducted by a small fraction of the traffic participants. Moreover, the intermediation of a central party is needed for the distribution of the data. Such central processing can cause significant delays, a factor which should not be neglected in traffic information systems.

2.2.4 Cooperative traffic information systems

An obvious extension of the aforementioned systems is to allow *all* participants to contribute their measurements of the traffic situation in their vicinity. Quite a large number of traffic information systems utilize this strategy: we call such systems *cooperative* traffic information systems. When communication becomes possible between the participants, they are able to conduct the measurements and share them with others. In this case the architecture of the traffic information systems (Figure 2.1) is simplified: the participants become mobile traffic sensors.

The main differences between the cooperative systems presented in the remainder of this section involve the way the measurements are exchanged between the participants. The first group uses direct communication between cars via wireless ad-hoc networks (called Vehicular Ad-Hoc Networks (VANETS)). A standard exists for such direct communication: DSRC [DSR03]. We will describe the idea and technical specification of VANETs in the next chapter. For now it is only necessary to state that the capacity and bandwidth offered by VANETs is limited. To cope with these problems almost all VANETs solutions try to reduce the amount of data that need to be transmitted. As we will show a reduction can be achieved by different means and is generally called aggregation of measurements.

One of the first of such a VANET-TIS was the Self Organizing Traffic Information System (SOTIS) [WER+03]. The authors of SOTIS assumed that each car is able to determine its position (by means of GPS), is equipped with a digital radio (for data exchange) and a digital map (serving as a common addressing scheme). The system was evaluated in simulations mainly in highway scenarios. In order to account for the limited bandwidth and capacity offered by VANET, information dissemination is used based on periodic local broadcasts and the store-and-forward principle. Each system participant maintains a local *knowledge base* consisting of its own measurements and data received from other users. The content of the knowledge base is used to prepare beacon packets (periodic reports). Such beacons are sent with a fixed interval and in addition to the content of the local knowledge base they also include their own traffic measurements. A single measurement is composed of the current position, velocity, heading and timestamp. To cope with the limited bandwidth of ad-hoc wireless networks, the authors proposed to merge the individual observations regarding the same fixed, pre-defined distant regions into one value. For each segment an average speed value $\bar{v}_s$ is sent. As soon as a new value (v_s) describing a given segment is available both are merged in the local knowledge base by using the following formula:

$$\bar{v}_{s,new} = (1-\alpha)\cdot \bar{v}_{s,prev} + \alpha \cdot v_s,$$

where $\alpha \in [0,1]$ is a pre-defined system constant. The authors claim that the reduction of detail in more distant regions reduces bandwidth consumption, while at the same time the most important information (i. e., descriptions of the immediate vicinity), is still available at a high level of detail. It is important to notice that the process of aggregation reduces the spatial and temporal resolution of the exchanged information and thus reduces the usability of the solution.

The idea of aggregation has also been followed by the authors of the next VANET-based system: TrafficView [NDLI04a]. TrafficView allows vehicles to exchange packets containing the following pieces of information:

- sender ID,

- position (POS),

- speed (SPD),

- broadcast time (BT),

to enable each individual vehicle to assess traffic and road conditions in front of it and react accordingly. Dissemination (here called diffusion) has been used for data exchange. Similar to SOTIS, after the reception of a broadcast from another car, the information is included in a local database but retransmission is deferred until the next broadcast period of the receiver. The authors compared this mechanism to classical flooding, where beacons are sent immediately after a new measurement has been created and are forwarded to reach all the participants in the network. The conclusion was that dissemination offers a much better gain/cost ratio for small equipment ratios and flooding does not scale well with an increasing number of equipped cars.

The application workflow involves the following steps: reception of the beacons, validation of the included data (duplicates, information from "behind the car" and obsolete data are removed), update of the local database, sending of aggregated data. The aggregation algorithm divides the road in front of the vehicle to a number of regions r_i. To each region, an aggregation ratio a_i is assigned. The aggregation ratio is defined as the inverse of the number of individual records that would be aggregated in a single record. The aggregation ratios and number of regions are assigned according to the importance of the regions and the required accuracy of the information. For instance creating equally-sized regions with decreasing aggregation ratios will result in broadcasting less accurate information about distant regions (similarly to SOTIS). All records $(ID_i, POS_i, SPD_i, BT_i)$ from a given region r_i are combined to form an aggregated record in the form of $((ID_1, ID_2, \ldots), POS_a, SPD_a, BT_a)$, where:

$$BT_a = min(BT_1, BT_2, \ldots),$$
$$POS_a = \sum POS_i/d_i,$$
$$SPD_a = \sum SPD_i/d_i$$

(d_i is the distance between the information originator and the aggregating car). The very basic idea of this aggregation scheme is that records generated by cars close to each other are similar and thus can be replaced by a single record with little error. The authors acknowledge the fact that in the case when very detailed information is available for one segment and only partial for the others, the detailed information will be lost in the aggregation process.

While the original information from which the aggregated record is produced is not transmitted, it is hard (or impossible) for other cars to remove old information from the record. The reason for that is the employed lossy compression of data. The information aging is realized in the following way: if the broadcast time of the records is greater than the broadcast time of the stored record, it means the new record is more recent, and therefore the node removes the corresponding vehicle ID from its stored record. In contrast, if the car has information with a smaller BT it discards the complete incoming record. Such an approach is not optimal. Apart from limited simulation evaluation of their solutions in a highway scenario, the authors have also undertaken some work towards prototype implementation.

StreetSmart [DJ07] deals with the limited capacity of VANETs in a different way. This system does not exchange information on *every* section of the road but rather focuses on areas of unexpected traffic. The authors claim that these regions are the most important for good routing decisions. The participating cars need not communicate if the vehicle is traveling at, or above the speed limit on the current road (so-called *need to say* principle). The detection of congested road segments is performed by a clustering algorithm (k-means). After sampling the data, nodes exchanging messages then each node merges their snapshot of other nodes centroid data with its local centroid. The distance between the points is calculated along the roads and not as a geographical distance. The presented solution uses sophisticated filtering to reduce the bandwidth usage. It should be stressed that extensive filtering of the data is a solution to the same problem as the aggregation schemes presented above: the collected data need to be distributed among multiple participants, and it also reduces the quality of the exchanged information (by discarding many measurements).

Another VANET-based traffic information system was presented in [LSW+08]. The paper presents a scalable aggregation scheme. The basic idea is as follows: a common digital street map is divided into a hierarchical set of landmarks. These are predefined and commonly known. At the highest level of the hierarchy there are junctions of the main roads or highways. Lower levels include all higher level landmarks and intersections of smaller streets. The lowest level consists of the complete road network. Cars passing a road segment make an observation of the current travel time between two neighboring low-level landmarks. This information is distributed within the closest surroundings. The observations from the lowest level are used to calculate travel times between landmarks of the next higher level (by summarizing the travel times in the area). This less detailed picture of travel times is distributed across a larger area than the observations of individual cars. From less detailed observation travel times are calculated and exchanged between landmarks of the next higher level of the hierarchy. The authors claim that by doing so, one can limit the size of data packets exchanged between the cars and use the broadcast medium more efficiently. Another important contribution of this paper is the assessment of the efficiency of data dissemination in the VANET network. The authors argue that at least in the roll-out phase of VANET additional support of road-side units (RSU) would be advisable for data exchange, otherwise high latencies might occur. Such RSUs clearly increase the deployment costs of the system.

From the idea of supporting communication in VANETs with infrastructure it is a short way to the use of common cellular communication for exchanging data between cars. We were the first to put this idea forward in [RSK+07]. Cellular infrastructure-based communication networks (like UMTS or GSM) allows us to avoid store-and-forward communication and the resulting delays that are inherent to all VANET-based approaches, and therefore has the potential to offer better service to the user. Compared to the previously mentioned TomTom HD Traffic, which also uses cellular networks to estimate the traffic conditions in a given region, we will rather follow the principle of cooperative traffic information systems, and allow users to share direct measurements of traffic conditions.

The original idea gathered momentum and further UMTS-based solutions were presented. For instance in [SSC+10], the feasibility of UMTS TIS was examined. The authors followed a centralized approach, in which cars use the Fast Traffic Alert Protocol (FTAP) in a UMTS network to send their observations about the current traffic conditions to a TIC (Traffic Information Center). The information is then processed and aggregated to generate a higher-level view of the traffic conditions. Usually data exchange in UMTS networks is realized via Dedicated Channels (DCH). The authors also examined possibilities of using the Random Access Channel (RACH) to exchange a small amount of information. Normally RACH is only used only for requesting and establishing DCH communication. However, a modification of the protocol allowed to send a small amount of data in RACH requests. As soon as the central processing is completed, all the participating cars are informed. This is accomplished by a multicast service built upon the UMTS Forward Access Channel (FACH). Messages sent via FACH can be received by all mobile stations in a cell. Therefore, it is used to implement the UMTS Multimedia Broadcast Multicast Service (MBMS). All communication within the system is IP-based, with single pieces of information exchanged in the form of small XML documents. It should be stressed that this system is feasible only if the operator of the UMTS network cooperates with the system deployer, allowing it to use the multicast functionality of UMTS and modified RACH protocol. The specific implementations of UMTS networks differ with regard to MBMS support. Therefore, the authors also included simulations of multicast realized by unicast. In such a scenario cars are informed via independent DCH channels. The measured network load was obviously higher than in the case where MBMS was used (2 000 kB/s and 2.5 kB/s respectively). An alternative approach would be to allow for reactive communication instead of using multicast: each node could then fetch only the data relevant to it. The authors, however, did not examine such an approach. In addition, due to the need of a tight cooperation between the system operator and network operator the number of potential participants is limited to the group of customers of a particular network operator.

2.3 Measurements

So far we have used the rather enigmatic term traffic measurements to describe the data that are exchanged and made available in a TIS. Let us review what is typically taken as a measurement of the traffic situation in the systems mentioned above. In [GIO04] a static digital map is organized into segments (sections between two successive highway exit points or junctions), and each time a segment is passed the measured travel time is published. Also [XB06] uses traveling times and a common digital map as a basis for TIS. In SOTIS [WER+03] rather the average speed on a given segment is measured and published in the system. Similarly, TrafficView [NDLI04a] uses the average speed on a street segment as the basis traffic measurement. Given a common street map both approaches are essentially equivalent to each other. By using a well known physical formula traveling time can be derived from a given average speed. To estimate the travel time along a segment, each participant only needs a common electronic map (to define the borders of a segment), and GPS to determine the position and current time. GPS is also able to measure the current velocity of a vehicle.

The process of routing decision with available dynamic information on traffic conditions has been examined in [WBKS02]. The authors discussed the cost functions that the traffic information should optimize. When traffic information is used to minimize the individual traveling times of the participants (that is provide them with the fastest route to the planned destination), it is sufficient to exchange information about the average travel times along the segments and make a decision based on the gradient of the reported values. But an application of traffic information systems as traffic control systems is also conceivable. Here it is rather an optimal traffic flow in the street network that is sought after. The authors have shown that information about the traffic density on street segments is needed in order to provide an optimal utilization of the street network. Chapter 7 of this thesis is devoted to the problem of dynamic routing.

2.4 Communication paradigms

Regardless of the source of traffic information and the underlying communication network, there are few possible communication paradigms applicable for the exchange of traffic-related information. In a general case we can distinguish between communication between the network of traffic sensors and the TIS and between the participants and the TIS. Since we shall use measurements made by the participants themselves there is no need to distinguish between these two actions: the same communication means will be used for collecting and distributing the measurements.

First, a very straightforward way of interacting with the traffic information system is to "flood" the measurements in the network so that all the participants receive them. In this scheme the measuring party sends its measurement in a broadcast fashion immediately after the measurement is conducted. Each receiving participant forwards the message further so that eventually all the users are informed. This is a valid paradigm in many VANET-based applications and thus also a natural candidate for the TIS. However, the scalability of such a solution is limited. In particular, there exits a danger of a so-called broadcast storm [NTCS99]. The paper shows that if there is no coordination between rebroadcasting parties it is possible to overload the network with redundant retransmission, inhibiting the distribution of new messages.

A more sophisticated way of exchanging data in a traffic information system is *dissemination*, which we described in the previous section. Here the parties also use a broadcast medium to exchange data but instead of publishing or forwarding the information immediately some sort of processing is performed. Each participant maintains a view of the current traffic conditions. This view is updated as soon as new information is available either by means of individual measurements or via reception of an external beacon. The view is used to produce a regular broadcast in the form of a beacon. Each beacon reflects the status of the traffic known to the sender. By sending individual measurements aggregated together with data obtained from other participants the usage of the medium can be optimized at the extent of reducing the level of detail offered. Small frequencies for periodic beacons have to be set for systems with a high number of participants.

Both paradigms presented so far were proactive paradigms. That is, they aimed at bringing all the measurements to all the participants, regardless if they needed them or not. It was impossible to fetch particular pieces of information explicitly; one rather had to receive all the data and "hope" that the relevant data were also included. The request/reply paradigm enables a different strategy. Here each participant can and must explicitly fetch data relevant to its routing decision, which reduces the amount of data that needs to be processed.

It is also conceivable to allow the traffic information system to "pull" the data [Rot09], for instance when the update frequency of a car or traffic sensor is too small and some data are instantly needed. The request is sent to the respective party (a car or stationary sensor), a measurement is conducted and the results are immediately sent back to the request's initiator.

Request/Reply allows explicit retrieval of the relevant data. But as long as retrieval of dynamic data is concerned, this approach has some shortcomings. In order to follow the development of the traffic conditions one would have to request the relevant data periodically. The shorter the intervals, the better and more up-to-date would be the local view of the traffic conditions. But what about a case where the relevant data do not change over time? The requesting party does not know that, or, more precisely, it learns about it after the data have been fetched and the communication resources have already been wasted in a redundant effort. The publish/subscribe paradigm can mitigate the problem. It decouples the process of publishing the content from the process of distributing it among the participants. This time an instance interested in some particular data has to register its interest in the system and as soon as new data matching its interest are available, the system will inform all the interested participants. Unless new data are available no communication effort will be undertaken.

2.5 System specification

Let us now summarize the design details of traffic information systems. A cooperative TIS is essentially a set of shared traffic-related information, along with mechanisms to access, use, and update it. In this thesis we focus on the case where the shared information serves as a basis for so-called dynamic routing. That is, it provides the driver with information about the current traffic situation along the planned route and allows determining an optimal routing decision, avoiding traffic jams and other unexpected deterioration. We assume that all participants are equipped with:

- a GPS receiver (or other means to determine the position and speed),
- a common digital street map,
- and a communication channel between the participants.

By means of the GPS receiver and electronic map, cars can determine their position and routes to the planned destination. Digital maps are also used as a basis for addressing road segments. A road segment is the part of a road between two consecutive intersections. In a street map, each road segment is uniquely identified by a globally known ID. The combination of GPS and map data allows each car to determine the ID of the road segment it is currently traveling on, and the IDs of the road segments it intends to pass along its future route. For these segments it is possible to retrieve the descriptions of the current traffic state. Each user will publish the observed travel times for each segment they drive through.

In our system we will use travel times as a basis traffic measurement and individual travel times as a metric to assess the quality of the solution. From the measurements also traffic density on a particular street and the gradients of both values (when needed) can be derived.

Our design is based on the cooperative effort of the participants to collect the data. Each participant will report its measured travel time on a segment basis: as soon as a car has traversed a road segment it contributes a measurement of its travel time along that segment. In exchange for contributing the measurements, the drivers receive the measurements made by other drivers.

Usually, a car's navigation system will obtain (actively or passively by means of different communication paradigms) the relevant data at the beginning of a journey. This includes measurements describing the current situation along the possible routes connecting the origin and the intended destination. On the basis of this data, the navigation system will be able to choose a good route with respect to the expected travel time and potentially other aspects determined by the driver's preferences. Since the traffic conditions change over time, it should be possible for the driver to follow the development of the traffic situation not only on the current path but also on alternate paths to the destination. By keeping in touch with the development it is possible to adapt the chosen route on the fly. We focus mainly on the traffic information system for a city scenario. Although the subject of traffic information systems has received a lot of attention, there is no working solution on the market that can enable dynamic navigation in the cities. Our system will store the data for a limited geographical area (like one city). We envision independent systems for each city.

Chapter 3

Vehicular Ad-Hoc Networks

The previous chapter has presented a large body of research on traffic information systems, among them solutions using direct communication between cars via Vehicular Ad-Hoc Networks. The idea of cars communicating with each other has been around for many years; the subject has become quite complex, with traffic information systems being only one of several applications envisioned for inter-vehicular communication. Thus at the beginning of this chapter we list the most important research projects in this field, their main goals and achievements. This should provide the reader with a basic understanding of the current state of the research on VANETs. Subsequently we will present and classify a number of proposed car-to-car applications. In addition, we will also discuss the distinct communication requirements and possible realization technologies for each classified group. This thesis focuses on applications from one group, i.e., traffic efficiency applications, and so implementation issues for this type of application will be presented in more detail, in particular the limited connectivity and capacity offered by VANETs. The network limitations discussed here will constitute the basis for our subsequent work on VANET-alternative approach presented in the further chapters.

3.1 Research projects on inter-vehicular communication

Let us first present the most important research and industry efforts toward Inter-Vehicular Communication (IVC), and Vehicular Ad-Hoc Networks in particular. We list the most significant projects in a chronological order. Probably the oldest currently running project dealing with car-to-car communication is the Intelligent Transportation System (ITS) Standards Program [U.S]. Founded in 1996 by the U.S. Department of Transportation (U.S. DOT), Federal Transit Administration and American Public Transportation Association, the ITS Standards Program has undertaken a range of activities to increase road safety and reduce traffic congestion by using information technology. First and foremost, ITS SP provides technical assistance to ITS deployers of all kinds, by supporting them with up-to-date information about ITS standards development, testing and deployment [U.S]. From a researcher's point of view however, the most important activity of the ITS is its attempt at developing and implementing standards and protocols to promote compatibility among different intelligent vehicle-highway systems technologies. The ITS Standards Program has also taken a step further in its support of the development of international ITS standards within the International Standards Organization (ISO) and Federal Communications Commission (FCC). The joint effort of these parties has resulted in the Dedicated Short Range Communications Standard (DSRC) [DSR03], which is a physical layer specification for future car-to-car and car-to-infrastructure communication. While the standard is similar to consumer Wireless LAN, it has been modified to account for the special needs of inter-vehicular communication. It uses a 75 MHz band either at a 2.5 GHz or 5 GHz frequency at the relatively high sending power of 2 W (significantly higher than the usual 100 mW of consumer WLAN). The maximal communication range is estimated to about 1000 m. Cars can communicate with each other or with static nodes called Road Side Units (RSU). So-called multi-hop communication is employed to transport information at higher ranges: the data packets sent by the originator are rebroadcast by the receivers so that more and more distant cars can be reached. Since there is no need for a communication infrastructure as the participants form an ad-hoc network each time information needs to be transmitted, the approach is often called Vehicular Ad-Hoc Networks (VANETs).

The first significant effort of European researchers toward car-to-car implementation was the FleetNet [Enk03] project. The project was founded in 2000 by the German Ministry of Education and Research (BMBF) and incorporated industry representatives (e. g., Daimler-Chrysler, NEC, Siemens, Bosch) and universities (Mannheim, Hamburg, Hanover and Brunswick). The objective was to improve the driver's and passenger's safety by using wireless Vehicular multi-hop Ad-hoc Networks for inter-vehicle communication. The main achievement was the development of routing protocols for VANETs. In particular, so-called geographical routing and contention-based forwarding were implemented and tested on a small scale with six Smart cars [FKM$^+$03]. The idea of geographic routing is based on the observation that most of car-to-car applications involve actions such as informing all the cars in a given region about a danger or traffic conditions. Usually the originator of the information does not know, and does not have to know, the exact identities of cars in a given area; thus instead of addressing them individually it rather uses their geographical positions.

A direct successor of FleetNet is the Car-2-Car Communication Consortium (C2CCC). It is a non-profit industrial-driven international organization initiated by European vehicle manufacturers and supported by equipment suppliers, research organizations (among them also Heinrich Heine University of Düsseldorf) and other partners. The main objective of the C2CCC is to increase road traffic safety and efficiency by means of cooperative Intelligent Transport Systems, with inter-vehicle communications supported by vehicle-to-roadside communications (also called car-to-x-communication or C2X). The consortium works in close cooperation with European and international standardization organizations, in particular U. S. ITS, on the development and release of an open European standard for IVC. The consortium continues the work of FleetNet to prove the technical feasibility of inter-vehicular communication [C2C]. Furthermore, realistic deployment strategies and business models are developed within the C2CCC to speed up market penetration. This is a very important, even if not technical, aspect of IVC: most of the proposed applications work properly if the ratio of equipped cars is significant. Equipped cars are needed to obtain and transport data by forming an ad-hoc network. The first buyers will, therefore, not profit directly from purchasing cars equipped with the new technology. In the C2CCC project marketing strategies are developed to deal with this hurdle.

The project eSafety [eSa], which was founded in 2002 by the European Commission, sets out the ambitious target of halving the number of road fatalities by the year 2020. This is supposed to be achieved by an increased effort of all safety stakeholders to accelerate the development, deployment and use of Intelligent Vehicle Safety Systems. A part of eSafety project is Sevecom (SEcure VEhicle COMmunication) [LBH+06], which deals with system security, a prerequisite for the successful deployment of all vehicular communication systems. In the case of inter-vehicular communication, sending data packets can influence the behavior of a driver. Thus it is essential to make sure that life-critical information is trustworthy and cannot be modified by an attacker. At the same time, the privacy of the drivers and passengers should be protected. The problem is rather challenging due to the specific properties of the operational environment (moving vehicles, sporadic connectivity, far-reaching decentralization etc.). GeoNet [Geo], another part of the eSafety project, will bring the basic results of the work of the Car-2-Car Communication Consortium to the next step by improving the specifications and creating basic software implementations of the proposed protocols and applications. The goal of GeoNet is to implement and formally test a networking mechanism in the form of standalone, ready-to-deploy software modules.

In 2008 the project sim^{TD} [sim] was founded (sim^{TD} stands for *Safe and Intelligent Mobility: Test Field Germany*). As the name implies, the main goal of this project is, in addition to further work on technological standards, to plan and conduct large-scale field tests of the IVC. The overall sim^{TD} test fleet comprises an internal fleet with up to 100 controlled test vehicles as well as an external fleet with approximately 300 vehicles. During the project a list of car-to-car and car-to-x applications will be standardized, implemented and tested either with DSRC [DSR03] or UMTS. Since the sim^{TD} project is pursuing quite ambitious

Table 3.1: Important Inter-Vehicular Communication Projects.

Name	Founded	Objectives/Achievements
ITS	1996	DSRC PHY Standard
FleetNet	2000	routing, small scale experiments
C2CCC	2002	cooperative ITS, standardization, deployment strategies
eSafety	2002	reduce the number of casualties, standardization
Sevecom	2005	secure the C2C communication
sim^{TD}	2008	implementation and large-scale field tests of the IVC

objectives, this required the involvement of government institutions (German Ministry of Economics and Technology (BMWi), German Federal Ministry of Education and Research (BMBF)), automotive companies (Daimler, Volkswagen, Fiat and others), the telecommunication industry (T-Mobile) and academia representatives (including Heinrich Heine University of Düsseldorf).

3.2 Applications overview

Table 3.1 summarizes the main goals and achievements of the research projects dealing with inter-vehicular communication. As a result of the research a long list of proposed car-to-car applications has emerged. We have already presented a traffic efficiency application, i.e., a cooperative traffic information system; VANETs and Inter-Vehicular Communication are also used as a basis for other applications. Since the main motivation of the C2C research projects was to increase road safety and efficiency and to create added value for the purchasers of IVC equipped cars, we will look more closely at the most prominent applications coping with this particular problems. We divide the applications in three groups: road safety applications, traffic efficiency applications and value-added applications. Such classification is often employed in the literature, e.g., [KRM07]. In addition, we will characterize each application group with respect to its unique communication patterns and demands.

3.2.1 Road safety applications

According to the statistics provided by the C2CCC [C2C] the main reasons for accidents involving an injury were driver error (86.1% of all cases) and in 5.1% road conditions. The former group can be split further: in 26.1 % of the cases the driver was driving too fast or was too close to avoid the accident, in 22.8 % of the cases the reason for the accident was a violation of the right of way, and in 11.1 % of the cases the driver took a wrong lane or chose a wrong overtaking maneuver. It is commonly believed that it is precisely in these cases that supporting the driver with new technology can help avoid accidents. The first possibility that constitutes an improvement in this field is to equip cars with sensors such as infrared cameras, radars, etc., in order to extend the local awareness of the driver. While the effort to equip cars with more and more sensors is currently underway, a new idea has been born: the limited range of on-board sensors can be extended by inter-vehicular communication. Individual vehicles could exchange their measurements, thus enlarging the sector around the vehicle that is covered by the sensors of a single car. This often allows counteracting critical situations by means of an informed and— in the true sense of the word— foresighted way of driving. Such applications are called safety applications. Let us now examine some examples of this kind of applications.

In Cooperative Collision Warning Systems (CCW) [EGH$^+$06, XMKS04] cars perform a periodic broadcast of small packets containing their current positions, speeds and heading vectors. This information is then processed to increase the driver's awareness of the situation in direct vicinity. The driver is warned if a dangerous situation is discovered. More specifically, CCW applications include Forward Collision Warning (FCW), Lane Change Assistance (LCA), and Electronic Emergency Brake Light (EEBL). In FCW, a vehicle uses the received messages to calculate the likelihood of a collision with the vehicle driving in front of it. Similarly, in EEBL the received messages are analyzed to determine if one or more leading vehicles are braking. In LCA a vehicle computes the future trajectory of the surrounding cars based on the available status messages in order to determine the likelihood that the vehicles will enter its path. If any of these applications detects a danger (the calculated likelihood is too high), the driver is informed and he or she has to undertake appropriate actions.

In [RCCL06] Robinson et al. identified further safety applications including Intersection Violation Warning, Traffic Signal Violation, Curve Speed Warning, Left Turn Assist and Stop Sign Assist. They also examined what information is needed by particular safety applications and came to the conclusion that some data (for instance the current position of a car) are broadcasted and utilized by many safety applications. The DSRC standard includes a list of messages and sensor information which are exchanged between cars, of which probably the most important ones are acceleration, heading, speed, UTC time and position [RCCL06]. Thus it is required that each vehicle possesses some type of localization device (e.g., GPS) to obtain the data. In some cases information from on-board sensors is also sent to other vehicles, for example the Anti-Lock Brake (ABS) state, steering wheel angle, and traction control state. In order to obtain this data the safety application has to be able to access the so-called *car information bus*. If the safety applications run independently some of the data will be sent many times, resulting in suboptimal medium usage. The authors proposed a solution called Flexible Message Dispatcher (FMD), which coordinates all these different applications and filters redundant information while providing the required frequency and accuracy of the information.

The intersection collision warning system [NNP+09] has been developed to exchange status information (including position, speed and heading) between cars approaching an intersection. The drivers are given a "cross traffic" warning when there is a vehicle simultaneously entering the intersection from a cross street. This is a typical example of extending the awareness of the driver: even if other cars remain unseen, information about a possible collision can be extracted from the information exchanged. The coordination of traffic lights proposed in [DKKS05] was an extension of the original idea of intersection assistance. The protocol informs all participants about the current status of the traffic light but also enables emergency cars to influence the lights when needed. An example scenario would be to switch the traffic light to green for a passing emergency car. This application is a good example showing that at least in some cases an interaction with intelligent infrastructure is both required and beneficial.

In [MCC+09] an after-crash driver warning system has been examined. This application comes into action after the collision has taken place. Warning packets sent by the damaged vehicles are broadcasted and forwarded by means of flooding in the nearby area to inform other cars about the danger. Whenever a car receives such a message for the first time it rebroadcasts it to all its direct neighbors, allowing the drivers additional time for proper decision making and potential maneuvers.

Also [KOKM10] presented an application which relies on intelligent infrastructure and will be mainly used in after-crash scenarios. The authors conducted a real-world evaluation of C2X Road Side Warning Devices, i. e., intelligent warning triangles. Such warning triangles would be equipped with communication devices to extend their functionality. It will no longer be necessary to see the triangle as the cars will have received the information sent by the triangle and informed the driver even before the actual triangle can be seen.

Summary

In each of the safety applications status messages must be transmitted quickly and reliably between the participants within a given geographical area. The area where the information is relevant is usually small. The most commonly used communication standard is direct communication between cars by way of DSRC [DSR03], but in some applications (like intersection collision warning) also car-to-infrastructure communication is utilized. For this applications neither routing nor explicit addressing of the message receivers is needed. Instead, the parties involved periodically broadcast small status messages to all the vehicles in transmission range. The neighboring vehicles process these messages, account for the information included and in some cases rebroadcast the original message. So far safety applications are discussed almost exclusively in the context of VANETs.

3.2.2 Traffic efficiency applications

We have already discussed extensively an example of a Traffic Efficiency Application, i.e., Traffic Information System. Another example of an application optimizing the traffic flow involves the guidance to available parking lots [CGM06]. A driver provided with such knowledge can plan his or her route accordingly and not waste time and fuel searching for free parking places. A solution presented in the paper is based on the data exchanged between vehicles and parking automats. Due to the limited capacity of VANETs, which we will discus in a more detailed manner later in this chapter, it is impossible to provide highly detailed up-to-date information to all vehicles. The authors acknowledge the fact and use aggregation to reduce the amount of data exchanged in the network. Each driver has exact information only about his or her direct vicinity and less exact data about more distant areas. The level of detail is inversely proportional to the distance within the described area. Atomic information in the system represents the availability of free parking places coordinated by one parking automat, whereas aggregated information represents summarized information about an area covering more than one parking automat. Each vehicle starts with an empty cache, i.e., it has no information about the free parking lots. During the trip, it receives reports from parking automats passed by and encountered vehicles. The received reports are integrated into the vehicle's cache and periodically broadcasted. The authors claim that this will allow providing a working system even when only a small number of cars is equipped. A similar approach was presented in [PTSP07], where the entire parking area in each city was divided into a large number of overlapping circular zones based on the density of parking lots. The data on parking lot usage in each zone were handled by road-side units, that is intelligent parking automats. The automats were inter-connected and performed a periodic broadcast. The cars passing by received information and could react accordingly. By employing RSUs the latency of information distribution is reduced. It is no longer needed for cars to transport information between distant regions by means of locomotion and multi-hop communication, but rather a backbone network is used for this purpose. Of course using interconnected RSUs increases the cost of the system.

Summary

In traffic efficiency applications the participating cars are not only consumers of information but at least some of them also produce information by sharing their observations. An observation involves, for instance, a local measurement of the current traffic conditions or the number of currently free parking slots, which is then distributed to other vehicles. This results in a characteristic communication pattern. TIS usually require communication among many participants over relatively large distances that can span about ten kilometers in the case of a city scenario up to a hundred kilometers on highways. Hence the communication requirements of TIS applications are quite challenging: continuously updated data measured by a large number of network nodes are to be made available to many vehicles in a relatively large area. Later in this chapter we will answer the question whether VANETs are suitable to handle such a challenging communication pattern.

3.2.3 Value-added applications

Although the popularity of VANETs is mainly driven by safety and efficiency applications, value-added applications constitute an important aspect of VANETs' market introduction. During a long journey passengers can be tired or bored, and this is where all kinds of games can make the journey more enjoyable. Secondly a unique characteristic of vehicular communication makes IVC an interesting platform for so-called *infotainment applications* and a platform for commercial activities which might play an important role in market introduction. Such services include, e. g., distribution of location-aware data about hotels, restaurants, local points of interest and leisure activities [C2C].

Another group of value-added applications are all kinds of multimedia streaming applications, for instance [SHF08]. Examples of multimedia content include multimedia advertisements or live audio broadcasts between drivers and passengers or traveling cars. In order to make the exchange efficient the authors proposed to use rateless codecs (fountain codes). In turn, emergency video streaming is an application at the border between value-added applications and security applications [PLO+06]. Multimedia data transmitted in the vehicular context will help enhance navigation safety; for example videos clips of an accident ahead of a driver will allow them to make a more informed decision regarding their route.

The last group of value-added applications for IVC are all kinds of games. These could be simple games like quizzes or crosswords [Pal07] played by the passengers of the cars traveling close to each other. But also more sophisticated massive mixed reality multi-player on-line games [TB10] have been proposed. The second paper envisioned games which will be context and location aware and they will take advantage of the inherent vehicular mobility by offering, for instance, special quests in given locations. It is however not clear if VANETs with their limited bandwidth and high latency can really serve as a solid basis for such games, especially since alternative mobile Internet access technologies have become reality today.

Summary

Value-added applications are viewed as an important factor supporting market introduction of VANETs. As already explained many safety and traffic efficiency applications rely on the fact that a substantial number of traffic participants are equipped with the technology. If the number of the equipped cars is small the quality of the service offered is limited. Thus there is a problem in how to introduce the VANET technology on the market. Simplifying to exaggeration, the car producers and VANET deployers have to answer the question: how to sell something which does not (initially) work? The financial burden of integrating the first VANET devices can be partially carried by the car manufactures. Applications like ad distribution allow us to hope that some third parties can also financially support the introduction, being motivated by the potential gains in the future. On the other hand, none of the value-added applications proposed so far demand VANETs; all of them can be, or already are, provided by mobile Internet access technologies available right now.

3.3 VANET limitations

This thesis deals with a concrete traffic efficiency application. As already pointed out, such applications rely on the exchange of up-to-date information between many participants spread over large geographical areas. So far such applications have mainly been discussed in the context of VANET. Here we argue that VANETs may not be the best network technology for traffic efficiency applications. The limitations of VANETs as far as traffic efficiency applications are concerned are twofold: on the one hand we have the problem of limited connectivity in ad-hoc networks resulting both from the small penetration ratio of the new technology and the inherent properties of car traffic flow. On the other hand, provided enough cars are equipped, the exchange of the data in VANETs is constrained by network capacity.

3.3.1 Limited connectivity

The problem of limited connectivity is a well-studied property of VANETs. The so-called network effect occurs in VANETs: if not enough cars are equipped the exchange of information is simply not feasible. The probability of having an equipped car in the direct vicinity is too small in the roll-out phase. For instance the authors of [KPDH08] warned that connectivity cannot be taken for granted in VANETs. They studied the problem of connectivity by means of both models and simulations, assessing the influence of factors such as car density, movement patterns, communication range, and placements of RSUs on the connectivity graph of a VANET. An important observation was that there are two distinct phases of connectivity: in a critical phase the vehicles form small clusters and are able to communicate within the clusters but the clusters are isolated. With increasing penetration ratio, the network switched to a super-critical phase and a giant cluster of all cars emerged, providing a connected graph. It is however important to notice that such a giant cluster emerged only when no traffic lights were used in the simulation, traffic lights lead to "clustering" by increasing the average distances between the cars (or clusters of cars).

An interesting interplay between car density and connectivity has been presented by the authors of [APR05]. They studied a simple highway scenario and showed that an increase in car density does not necessary result in a higher connectivity. This is a little counterintuitive. On the one hand a higher density clearly increases the probability of having an equipped neighbor within the communication range. Increasing the density beyond a critical value leads, however, to a situation when even small driving fluctuations may cause traffic jams and the distribution of nodes in VANETs becomes inhomogeneous, for instance if stop-and-go traffic occurs. The distances between cars increases beyond communication range and the connectivity drops (isolated car clusters occur). A rather pessimistic conclusion reached in the works listed above is that, due to the special properties of car traffic flow, even if all cars were equipped with the technology it would not always be possible to establish permanent connections between randomly chosen cars.

Since there is no guarantee of end-to-end connectivity between any two given cars in a VANET, the applications have to be built in a different fashion. Most of the convenient applications are built in such a way that no end-to-end connectivity is needed. Instead, a delay tolerant network (DTN) approach with proactive dissemination of the aggregated information is used. This is achieved in the following way: a car possesses some information (either its own measurements or measurements already received) and periodically broadcasts them to all cars in the direct vicinity. Information between distant clusters of cars is transported by means of vehicular movement. [LSCM07] addressed the question if such dissemination is feasible and what the speed and efficiency of the dissemination are depending on the number of equipped vehicles. They performed a full-fledged simulation in a realistic city scenario and showed that data exchange can take very long, especially in the roll-out phase of VANETs when only a limited number of cars are equipped. Even worse is the fact that for small penetration ratios, the number of cars possessing any knowledge about the current traffic conditions (besides their own measurements) falls very quickly with increasing distance to the information source. This fact may undermine the idea of traffic information systems: the navigation units will have to make an initial routing decision with no information about the current traffic conditions available. Thus the authors proposed to use inter-connected RSUs to support data distribution and make dissemination over large geographical areas feasible and efficient. The idea is simple: additional infrastructure constitutes "bridges" between natural clusters of cars allowing communication between distinct cars.

The idea of additional supporting communication in mobile networks was also examined in [BCTL08]. The study was intended to constitute the basis for a cost-benefit analysis of deploying VANETs. In particular, different kinds of supporting infrastructure were discussed: inter-connected base stations, wireless meshes and disconnected relays. From the proposed analytical model a conclusion was drawn that in order to improve the average packet delivery delay $\sqrt{N}$ (N-number of participants) interconnected base stations (RSUs) and even more relays had to be employed. Secondly, the authors admitted that a delay tolerant network approach used as a basis for the analysis can incur delays from seconds to hours or even days in information dissemination. In order to achieve delays of the order of seconds (which will be necessary for traffic information applications) an even larger number of inter-connected base stations are needed [BCTL08].

If VANETs require additional infrastructure to work, it might be, however, reasonable to use an existing infrastructure (like general purpose cellular communication networks) rather that building a new one exclusively for inter-vehicular communication.

3.3.2 Limited capacity

The limited capacity of the broadcast networks constitutes the second problem in the exchange of information between many parties spread over large geographical areas. Although there exists a large body of work regarding the feasibility and infeasibility of wireless multi-hop networks with regard to network capacity, to the best of our knowledge we were the first to study the theoretical background behind the capacity of VANETs [SLRM09]. While many aggregation mechanisms and applications based on aggregation have been proposed, for example [NDLI04b, CGM06, LSM07] mentioned above, little is understood yet about the fundamental limitations and requirements of VANET data aggregation. It has often been stated that aggregation is necessary for scalable VANET information dissemination. But what are the characteristics of suitable aggregation schemes? How frequently can updates of, for example, traffic information be provided to remote cars? By how much does one have to reduce the "resolution" of information about distant areas? Here we provide a formal framework for evaluating the scalability of a given aggregation scheme. We also assess the amount of aggregation which is needed to make an application scalable. This amount describes how much of the original data are lost when aggregation is employed.

As far as the capacity of static wireless ad-hoc networks is considered, a large body of theoretical work followed the milestone paper by Gupta and Kumar [GK00], who introduced a framework that has frequently been used since then. Their results in unicast communication have later been generalized to a broader class of communication patterns; for instance, Keshavarz-Haddad et al. [KHRR06] assess the capacity for broadcast communication, and Shakkottai et al. [SLS07] consider multicast. Wang et al. [WSGLA08] present generic results for a broader family of communication paradigms termed (n, m, k)-casting. In [KHR07], results for unicast, multicast and broadcast are derived based on a model that differs in a number of fundamental aspects from the one introduced by Gupta and Kumar. An important aspect in the context of our work is the distance between sender and receiver which is taken into account in the distance-weighed throughput metric used in [XK04]. For the specific case of VANETs,

Pishro-Nik et al. [PNGN07] assessed capacity scaling laws for unicast end-to-end communication and their dependency on the characteristics of the road network; within the same framework, distance-limited unicast and broadcast communication is analyzed in [NEPN08]. None of these works, however, is applicable to the questions posed here, because none of them considers any form of in-network aggregation which is widely used by traffic efficiency applications proposed so far. This section is meant as a step towards a deeper understanding of these fundamental issues.

Previous work has concerned individual, specific aggregation schemes and dissemination mechanisms, and has evaluated them in specific situations and environments, using simulations and experiments. Here we consider the generic class of *all* possible aggregation and dissemination mechanisms. We are interested in capturing the underlying effects and principles in order to derive general limits that *any* protocol design must respect. Consequently, our methodology of choice is not simulation or experimentation, but theoretical analysis.

VANETs, just like static wireless multi-hop networks mentioned above, also have a limited capacity. Hence, it is obviously impossible to send continuous updates about each location where measurements are taken to all network participants at a fixed data rate. It has thus been proposed to aggregate data in proportion to increasing distance, i. e., to maintain and distribute a detailed picture within the closer vicinity and coarser and coarser information about increasingly distant areas.

In order to deal with the broad range of conceivable aggregation schemes, we need a suitable abstraction that captures the essence of in-network data aggregation regardless how it is specifically performed. To this end, we introduce the notion of *bandwidth profiles*. Simply speaking (a rigorous definition will follow), a bandwidth profile of an aggregation scheme describes how rapidly the amount of information made available is reduced with increasing distance. As it turns out, bandwidth profiles constitute a valuable tool to describe the general properties of aggregation schemes; all our main results will be formulated in terms of bandwidth profiles.

Our primary focus is on the minimum aggregation requirements for scalable dissemination applications in two-dimensional wireless networks—a setting which satisfactorily describes VANET dissemination applications, like traffic information systems. We consider this from an asymptotic perspective, demonstrating that a network and application model with very weak assumptions already allows us to derive interesting results. Because our assumptions about the network are weak, the results are strong: the proofs hold for a broad class of protocols and aggregation algorithms.

In particular, we will show that any dissemination mechanism, in order to be scalable in a general setting, must reduce the bandwidth at which information about an area at distance d is provided to the cars asymptotically faster than $1/d^2$. This result does not depend on the *way* how this bandwidth reduction is achieved: it holds regardless of whether, for instance, information about distant roads, parking lots, etc. is updated at a lower frequency, whether data from multiple sources are summarized, whether less accurate (and thus more compact) data representations are employed, or whether some or all of these techniques are combined in order to reduce the utilized bandwidth. It also does not depend on the communication paradigm used for transporting the information, be it proactive or request-based, using unicast, multicast, broadcast, geocast, DTN-style opportunistic gossiping, or anything else.

Model

Let us first introduce the network and application model that we will use throughout the section. Our aim is to capture the relevant aspects of wireless networks in general and VANETs in particular, while keeping the focus of our assumptions on those factors that are later on essential for our proofs—each non-essential constraint in the model would unnecessarily limit the applicability and generality of the results. Specifically, our model comprises three components:

1. The sources of information, i.e., where the disseminated and aggregated data come from. Here, we call these sources *measurement points*.

2. Where the information goes, i.e., which information is to be delivered to which cars in the VANET. We term this relation the *interests* in the system.

3. The limitations on the propagation of information imposed by the network as a result of limited spatial reuse of the medium, in particular due to wireless interference.

Measurement points Our model represents the "world", i.e., the area the system is deployed on, by the real plane R^2. For practical purposes, this is a reasonable approximation of a city area, a country, or even a continent. On this plane, there is a set $M \subset \mathrm{R}^2$ of locations at which information can be obtained through measurements. These *measurement points* could, for example, represent all the street segments, for which passing cars would observe the current traffic density, driving velocity, number of free parking places, road surface condition, or any other parameter. The observed values are time-varying, i.e., the measurements are always taken at some specific time instant. Due to this temporal property, we see a measurement point as an information source that "produces" information about the measured value whenever a measurement is performed. Considered over a sufficiently long time span and seen from an abstract perspective, a measurement point thus is a source which generates information at a certain *data rate*. The task of an information dissemination protocol is to deliver this generated information to the interested network participants. The focus here is to assess the asymptotic limits of the rate at which information obtained from the measurement points can be *delivered* to interested cars, regardless of the specific protocols used to transport it and the in-network aggregation techniques used to achieve the desired rate.

While, at a first glance, this abstraction bears similarities with the existing work on asymptotic rate limits, there is one fundamentally distinctive aspect: with in-network aggregation, the data rate changes *within* the network. Typically, with increasing distance, the amount of information about a measurement point is reduced further and further, for instance by summarizing it with other data.

Generally, the achievable performance will depend on the distribution and density of the measurement points on the plane. If there are only a few measurement points, disseminating the information will be easier than in the case of a large number of information sources. We therefore have to model the spatial distribution of the measurement points. If we allow for arbitrarily large and dense clusters of measurement points, an arbitrarily large amount of information can be generated in a very limited area; then, their information can obviously not be communicated even locally and asymptotic bandwidth considerations become meaningless. However, since we intend to remain as generic as possible in our analysis, we impose only a very weak condition on the distribution of the measurement points. We concentrate on the case where the measurement point distribution satisfies what we call a *max-density condition*. This condition essentially states that there are no arbitrarily large, arbitrarily dense groups or clusters of measurement points. It is formally defined as follows:

Definition 3.1. *A set of measurement points M fulfills a max-density condition with parameters $\delta > 0$ and $r_0 > 0$ if and only if for any circle in $\mathbb{R}^2$ with radius $r \geq r_0$ the number ν of measurement points that lie within the circle is bounded above by*

$$\nu < \delta r^2.$$

Note that in the previous definition, parameter choices where $\delta r_0^2 \leq 1$ do not make sense, because they would not allow for even just one single measurement point to exist: let m be a measurement point and consider a circle with radius $r = r_0$ around m; this circle would contain one measurement point and would thus already violate a max-density condition with $\delta r_0^2 \leq 1$. Therefore, we may safely assume that δr_0^2 will always be larger than 1.

Interests The next aspect that needs to be modeled is the distribution of interests in the system: where does the information need to be delivered to? Or, more specifically, the question is which measurement points are the object of interest of cars in which particular region of the map? Clearly this aspect is highly application dependent. In a traffic information system, for example, cars will be interested in the traffic situation along their planned route; thus, the interests depend on the traffic movement pattern, and will typically include both close measurement points and much more distant road sections. Because our aim is to investigate the fundamental limits that hold for any application and any road network, our model deliberately does not constrain the possible distribution of interests in the system. We therefore model the interests of the participants in the dissemination system by an arbitrary set of pairs (x, m), where x is the location of a network participant that is interested in data from a measurement point $m \in M$. The formal definition is as follows.

Definition 3.2. *Let the interest set $\mathcal{I}$ be an arbitrary subset of $\mathbb{R}^2 \times M$.*

Since we are interested in the rate at which data about a measurement point can be made available given the distance between the measurement point and the interested car, we also introduce a notion for this distance:

Definition 3.3. *The distance $\|I\|$ of an interest $I \in \mathcal{I}$, where $I = (x, m)$, is the distance between the position of the interested party x and the measurement point m, i.e.,*
$$\|I\| := \|x - m\|.$$

Limitations of the network Finally, we have to consider the network capacity itself. In a network with unlimited capacity, it would not be a problem to deliver all measurement data about all measurement points to each interested participant. In practice, however, each network imposes limitations on the maximum bandwidth between communication partners. In wireless networks like VANETs, the central limiting factor are spatial reuse constraints due to signal interference. In order to obtain strong results, we again aim to capture the essence of these limitations in a way that is as generic as possible, with as few specifics of and assumptions about any particular network or communication mechanism as possible.

We again do so using circles on the plane. Any other shape would do equally well, but circles are particularly easy to handle. Our idea is sketched in Figure 3.1:

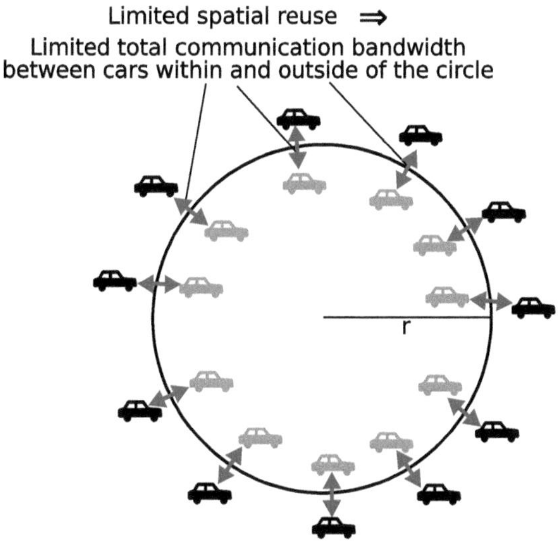

Limited spatial reuse ⇒
Limited total communication bandwidth
between cars within and outside of the circle

Figure 3.1: The total communication bandwidth into a circle of finite radius.

we place a circle with finite radius somewhere in our wireless network. If we add up all the bandwidth of all communication links crossing the circle boundary that we could possibly use in parallel, this sum will always be finite—wireless interference limits the spatial reuse. We thus cannot communicate an arbitrarily large amount of data into (or out of) our circle within a limited time.

We formalize this observation in the following assumption. Note that it only constitutes an upper bound; we do not assume that the maximum bandwidth is ever actually achieved.

Assumption 3.1. *Given any arbitrary radius $r > 0$, we assume that there is a constant ξ_r, such that for any circle with radius r, the total communication bandwidth b (observed over a reasonably long time span) between the nodes within and outside the circle is bounded above by*

$$b \leq \xi_r.$$

The total communication bandwidth between the inside and the outside of our circle (i.e., the constant ξ_r) will typically increase for larger radii r. However, we do not need to model this in detail: for our proof, it is sufficient that for any fixed, given radius, the total bandwidth may not become arbitrarily high.

Bandwidth Constraints for Scalable Aggregation

Before we turn to the question of *how much* aggregation is necessary, let us first argue—in terms of our model—why data aggregation is necessarily needed for dissemination services in VANETs *at all*. Consider a circle with arbitrary radius r around the participant's current position; according to Assumption 3.1 the total data rate of information from measurement points outside this circle provided to the participant cannot exceed ξ_r.

Grossglauser and Tse [GT02] and some subsequent works showed that— theoretically—the capacity of wireless networks increases if node mobility is taken into account. The results were, however, derived under assumption of unlimited buffer sizes and only guarantee the delivery of the message even with almost infinite delay. The mobility does not affect our results: it will only increase the data rate b at which the information can flow into the toe circle, as some information will travel on-board the incoming cars.

One approach would of course be to limit the number of interests. This, however, is hardly viable. It is of course possible to put a limit on the allowed number of interests of a single network participant; such a limit may even inherently exist in the application. Note, however, that it will often be the case that many network participants which are interested in very different regions are co-located within the same geographical area. For example, cars with very different destinations and different planned routes may be underway on the same road. However, despite the almost arbitrarily large variety of interests, the total ingress bandwidth for these cars is still limited. (In terms of our model, consider a circle enclosing all the cars, then the total bandwidth into this circle is limited.) Thus, a much more promising approach is to use in-network summarization and aggregation techniques to adjust the resolution of the provided information (and thus the necessary data rate) in order to respect the inherent bandwidth limitations of inter-vehicle communication.

Bandwidth profiles Aggregation techniques exist in many different shades and flavors. For instance, information from the measurement points within the same geographical area may be aggregated, such that only a summary is transmitted to interested parties further away, as it has been proposed in [CGM06, LSM07]; information from individual vehicles on a road may be combined as in [NDLI04b]; the frequency at which information about certain geographical regions is transmitted may be adjusted as in [KSA02]; syntactic compression techniques may be used to yield smaller aggregates, as suggested in [IW08b]; or travel times between important "landmarks" may be used as a coarser representation of the traffic situation at larger distances as has been proposed in [LSW+08].

All these techniques—more or less directly—aim at reducing the data rate used per measurement point with increasing distance of the interest, either by using coarser approximations of the value itself (i.e., data representations requiring fewer bits), by sending updates less often, or by transmitting one single value for a whole group of measurement points, which in the end also boils down to reducing the rate used per measurement point.

In our analytical approach to determine the fundamental limits of aggregation, we must find a way to abstract from the specific approaches and mechanisms of aggregation. We therefore identify the reduction of the data rate per measurement point with increasing distance as their common feature. From this point of view, the essential property of an aggregation scheme is the amount of bandwidth spent depending on the distance: given an interest with distance d, how much bandwidth is used for making information available to the interested party? Consequently, we characterize an aggregation scheme by its *bandwidth profile*.

Definition 3.4. *A monotonically decreasing function*

$$b: \mathrm{R} \to \mathrm{R}_{\geq 0}$$

is a bandwidth profile of an aggregation scheme $\mathcal{A}$ if $\mathcal{A}$ ensures that for all interests $I = (x, m) \in \mathcal{I}$ an interested party located at x is supplied with information about measurement point m at least with data rate $b(\|I\|)$.

Towards a proof In the remainder of this section, we will prove for the general case of arbitrary measurement point sets (with a max-density property) and interests that if an aggregation scheme has a bandwidth profile b for which $b(d) \notin o(1/d^2)$, then the bandwidth limitations established by Assumption 3.1 do not allow ensuring that all interests can be appropriately served.[1] I. e., we will prove by contradiction that all bandwidth profiles of scalable aggregation schemes must be in $o(1/d^2)$. Hence, practical aggregation schemes should be constructed in a way such that the data rate used per measurement point decreases faster than with the square of the interest's distance.

In the proof, we will make use of the following two lemmas.

Lemma 3.1. *Let $\delta > 0$, $r_0 > 0$ be given such that $\delta r_0^2 > 1$. If the measurement points in M are distributed in such a way that the distance between any two measurement points is at least*

$$\Delta := \frac{2}{\sqrt{\delta} - r_0^{-1}},$$

then a max-density condition with parameters δ and r_0 according to Definition 3.1 holds.

This lemma is proved in Appendix A.1.

Note that the condition in Lemma 3.1 is sufficient, but not necessary. In particular, we do not claim that measurement points will always have a pair-wise

---

[1] $o(1/d^2)$, not to be confused with $O(1/d^2)$, describes the set of functions which decrease asymptotically faster than $1/d^2$. More formally, $b(d) \in o(1/d^2)$ if and only if

$$\forall c > 0 : \exists d_0 > 0 : \forall d > d_0 : b(d) < \frac{c}{d^2}.$$

distance of Δ; we will just use this lemma as a vehicle to show that one specific distribution of measurement points (the counterexample in the proof by contradiction of our main theorem) fulfills a max-density condition.

Lemma 3.2. *On the perimeter of a circle with radius $r \geq \frac{\Delta}{2}$, at least $\lfloor \frac{4r}{\Delta} \rfloor$ points can be positioned such that for each pair of points their distance is at least Δ.*

The proof for this lemma can be found in Appendix A.2.

Constructing a counterexample In the following, we will assume that the parameters δ and r_0 from the max-density condition are fixed and given. Let furthermore Δ in the following denote the quantity $\frac{2}{\sqrt{\delta - r_0^{-1}}}$, as in Lemma 3.1.

We will now show that any bandwidth profile must be in $o(1/d^2)$, or otherwise there is a possible constellation of measurement points and interests such that a max-density condition holds, but not all interests I can be satisfied with data rate $b(\|I\|)$. We prove this by contradiction. Therefore, let from now on b be a bandwidth profile for which

$$b(d) \notin o\left(\frac{1}{d^2}\right). \tag{3.1}$$

We will proceed in three steps towards a proof. We first construct a set of measurement points M^* and set of interests $\mathcal{I}^*$ based on the parameters δ, r_0 from the max-density condition. We then show that for this construction the max-density condition holds. Finally, we prove that serving all interests $I \in \mathcal{I}^*$ with data rate at least $b(\|I\|)$ is not feasible.

Note that $b \notin o(1/d^2)$ means that there is a constant $c > 0$ such that

$$\forall d_0 > 0 : \exists d > d_0 : b(d) \geq \frac{c}{d^2}. \tag{3.2}$$

In the following, let c be such a constant.

Definition 3.5. *Let $k_0 := \max\{r_0, \Delta\}$.*

For all $i \in \mathbb{N}_{>0}$ let $k_i \in \mathbb{R}$ be a value for which

$$k_i > 8k_{i-1} + \Delta \quad \text{and} \quad b(k_i) \geq \frac{c}{k_i^2}.$$

Such k_i exists for all k_{i-1} because $b(d) \notin o(1/d^2)$ (to see this, set $d_0 = 8k_{i-1} + \Delta$ and $d = k_i$ in (3.2)).

Based on the sequence $(k_i)_{i \in \mathbb{N}}$ we can now construct the specific sets of measurement points M^* and interests $\mathcal{I}^*$ for our counterexample as follows.

Definition 3.6. *Let M^* be a set of measurement points defined as follows.*

We first construct a sequence of primary circles. The primary circles are all centered at the origin $(0,0)$. The i-th primary circle $(i \geq 0)$, denoted by $C_{i,0}$, has radius k_i.

For all $i \in \mathbb{N}_{>0}$ we construct further circles between the primary circles, in a way such that the radii of any pair of circles differ by at least Δ. We call these additional circles secondary circles. The secondary circles, too, are centered at the origin. Between $C_{i-1,0}$ and $C_{i,0}$, there are $w_i - 1$ secondary circles, denoted by $C_{i,1}, \ldots, C_{i,w_i-1}$, where

$$w_i = \left\lfloor \frac{k_i - k_{i-1}}{\Delta} \right\rfloor.$$

Let the radius of $C_{i,j}$ be $k_i - j\Delta$.

Figure 3.2 depicts the idea of primary and secondary circles (solid and dashed lines, respectively).

According to Lemma 3.2,

$$\left\lfloor \frac{4(k_i - j\Delta)}{\Delta} \right\rfloor$$

points can be positioned on $C_{i,j}$, such that they all have a pair-wise distance of at least Δ. M^* consists of such points on all circles $C_{i,j}$ where $i > 0$. The exact placement of the points on the circle is not relevant in the following, as long as the pair-wise distance is at least Δ; for instance, one point on $C_{i,j}$ could be

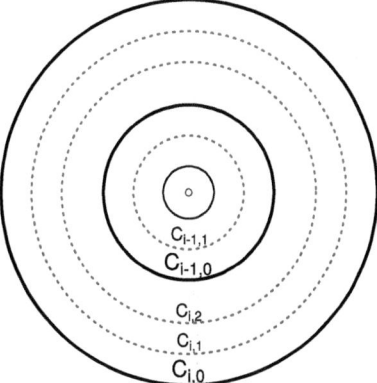

Figure 3.2: Primary and secondary circles in the construction of M^*.

positioned at coordinates $(0, k_i - j\Delta)$, with the rest of the points uniformly spaced over the circle perimeter.

Let the i-th zone, Z_i, be the subset of M^* that contains all measurement points residing on the circles $C_{i,0}, \ldots, C_{i,w_i-1}$ (i.e., it comprises the primary circle $C_{i,0}$ and all secondary circles between $C_{i-1,0}$ and $C_{i,0}$). Observe that the zones are all of finite size, are all pairwise disjoint, and together fully cover M^*. Let z_i denote the number of measurement points in zone Z_i.

Finally, let
$$\mathcal{I}^* = \{((0,0), m) \mid m \in M^*\}.$$

We must now verify that a max-density condition with parameters δ and r_0 holds for our construction.

Theorem 3.1. *A max-density condition with parameters δ, r_0 holds for M^*.*

Proof. We show that for any two measurement points $m_1, m_2 \in M^*, m_1 \neq m_2$ the distance $\|m_1 - m_2\|$ is at least Δ. First, note that according to Definition 3.6 the difference between the radii of any two circles is at least Δ. Therefore, if m_1

and m_2 reside on different circles, their distance must be at least Δ. If m_1 and m_2 are located on the same circle, however, their distance is also at least Δ by construction.

Consequently, the distance between any pair of measurement points is at least Δ. Thus, by Lemma 3.1, the max-density condition holds. $\square$

We now turn to the number of measurement points within the individual zones and make the following observation regarding the number of measurement points in a zone.

Lemma 3.3. *Let $i \in \mathbb{N}_{>0}$. For the number of measurement points z_i in zone Z_i it holds that*
$$z_i > \frac{k_i^2}{2\Delta^2}.$$

The lemma is proved in Appendix A.3.

A criterion for scalability Finally, we are ready to prove our main theorem, which characterizes the minimum "amount" of aggregation necessary for a scalable dissemination scheme.

Theorem 3.2. *Let b be an arbitrary bandwidth profile for which $b(d) \notin o(1/d^2)$. Then, for measurement points M^* and interests $\mathcal{I}^*$ as defined above, not all interests $I \in \mathcal{I}^*$ can be served with bandwidth at least $b(\|I\|)$.*

Proof. Let M^* and $\mathcal{I}^*$ be defined like above. Consider a circle C^* centered around 0 with radius $r^* := k_0/2$. Note that, by construction, all circles in the definition of M^* have a radius larger than r^*; thus, all points in M^* are located outside C^*. Since for each $m \in M^*$ there is an interest $I_m = ((0,0), m) \in \mathcal{I}^*$, information about m must be transported into C^* at least with data rate $b(\|I_m\|)$. Note that $\|I_m\|$ is equal to the radius of the measurement point circle (according to the definition of M^*) on which m is located.

Now observe that for each measurement point m in zone Z_i, the bandwidth that must be spent for the point when delivering information for interest I_m is bounded below as follows

$$b(\|I_m\|) \geq b(k_i), \qquad (3.3)$$

because b is monotonically decreasing per definition and $\|I_m\| \leq k_i$.

Therefore, the total rate B at which data must be transported into C^* to serve all interests according to b is—by summation over the zones—bounded below by

$$B \geq \sum_{i=1}^{\infty} b(k_i) z_i \geq \sum_{i=1}^{\infty} \frac{c}{k_i^2} z_i. \qquad (3.4)$$

According to Lemma 3.3, we thus have

$$B > \sum_{i=1}^{\infty} \frac{c}{k_i^2} \left(\frac{k_i^2}{2\Delta^2} \right) = \frac{c}{2\Delta^2} \sum_{i=1}^{\infty} 1. \qquad (3.5)$$

This sum obviously does not converge, therefore it would require infinite bandwidth into the circle C^* to serve all interests. Since the bandwidth available for transmissions into C^* is finite (bounded above by ξ_{r^*} according to Assumption 3.1), the assertion holds. □

Note that while from the above construction and proof it may seem that an infinite number of interests and measurement points is necessary in order to break a scheme with a bandwidth profile that is not in $o(1/d^2)$, this is not exactly true: one can always find a *finite* number of zones (and thus a finite number of measurement points and interests) for which the sum in (3.4) already exceeds the available bandwidth.

An example

Out of the many proposed aggregation schemes, let us pick SOTIS [WER+03] in order to show what our results mean in practice. As described in Section 2.2.4, in this approach when a vehicle receives a beacon containing information about traffic conditions, it merges the information into a local knowledge base, and sends out aggregated subsets of the information from its knowledge base in the beacons. SOTIS uses fixed-size road segments to summarize travel speeds provided by different participants.

Given its own position, each car then has a set of data elements that it can choose to report on. The car must decide on the subset of elements about which information (e.g., traffic measurement) is included in the beacons, and also *how often* it is included—in every beacon, in every other beacon, etc.. The choice can be captured by defining a (position-dependent) frequency f_E for each element E of the set, where a car includes information about E in its beacons with frequency f_E. These frequencies implicitly also determine the beaconing interval and the size of the beacons, and therefore the network bandwidth used.

Our previous results are directly applicable to such a model. If we assume, for simplicity of discussion, a constant density of measurement points and a constant aggregate size, we can obtain results on how we must choose the frequencies. From the results in Section 3.3.2, we learn that this can only be scalable if we reduce the rate like $o(1/d^2)$ over distance. With constant aggregate size, we would indeed need a quite rapid reduction of the frequency to achieve the necessary rate reduction—faster than $1/d^2$. When the transmission frequency is reduced so quickly for more distant regions, however, it might be questionable whether these rare transmissions of information about more distant segments can be practically useful at all: cars might barely be able to obtain useful information about more distant regions within reasonable time spans.

Scope and applicability

The results presented in this section shed light on an aspect that has so far been neglected in VANET data aggregation: the extent to which aggregation is needed. Of course, in practice, not only asymptotic scaling, as it is considered here, but also the constants involved will play a significant role; moreover, one must be aware of the fact that VANETs are large networks but cannot be extended infinitely. Therefore, in practice, careful consideration is inevitable, and application-specific aspects must be taken into account. VANET applications will be long-lived deployments, where the introduction of revised or even re-designed protocols is difficult or impossible. At design time, the detailed characteristics of all (road) networks in which an application will be used will typically be unknown; the same holds true for the future usage pattern of an application. The notion of a bandwidth profile and the results on the asymptotic scaling of aggregation schemes therefore constitute valuable guidelines when mechanisms for VANET dissemination applications are selected, adapted, or designed: such mechanisms should at least *allow* to avoid bandwidth profiles which are not in $o(1/d^2)$—otherwise they are bound to fail in the general case. Some, but not all of the existing mechanisms already provide the necessary flexibility. In any case, before aggregation mechanisms are considered as a basis for large-scale applications, they should be subjected to a rigorous analysis with respect to their bandwidth requirements and their scaling behavior.

On the one hand our results provide valuable hints on how specific aggregation mechanisms and VANET applications should be designed. On the other hand, the results might also be considered as an argument against using VANETs while designing inter-vehicular applications relying on exchange of data between many users in a large geographical area. Basically, in order to make a VANET application scalable, the designers have to either limit the number of participants, bound the geographical area the information is distributed in, or reduce the size (and level of detail) of the exchanged data. Each of these countermeasures limits the usability of the application.

3.4 Conclusion

In this chapter we presented research projects dealing with inter-vehicular communication and discussed proposed examples of car-to-car and car-to-x applications. For each application group we defined a set of unique communication requirements. This thesis focuses on the applications from the traffic efficiency group. Thus we also examined the suitability of VANETs when building such applications. The VANET approach incurs no additional cost for a driver in order to receive and use up-to-date information for his or her navigation. However, a difficult task when building such a system involves equipping enough cars with the technology. A sufficient performance is hard to reach, if not impossible, with penetration ratios that are realistic within the near future or during a roll-out phase. This might be mitigated by leveraging the VANET approach and using additional infrastructure support; however, the cost efficiency of such a solution is questionable.

Assuming the obstacles of market introduction are dealt with and a large fraction of cars are equipped with the technology still, due to the inherent characteristics of car movement, even with a significant number of cars equipped with the technology, there is no guarantee of end-to-end communication between any two cars in VANET. Thus the data has to be transported by being "carried" through the movement of a car; this, however, radically reduces the speed of dissemination.

Due to capacity limitations, dissemination-based applications in VANETs must involve the application of data aggregation techniques that reduce the amount of information with increasing distance. This chapter contains two central contributions with respect to a deeper understanding of the trade-offs of VANET-based communication: first, we introduced the concept of a bandwidth profile, and showed that aggregation schemes cannot be considered generally scalable unless their bandwidth profiles are in $o(1/d^2)$, where d is the geographical distance between a source of information and an interested vehicle. Aggregation of data always entails the loss of detail in the original data. It might happen that a scalable aggregation protocol results in exchange of data which are not useful for the application of dynamic routing. The data might be obsolete and not detailed enough to allow for good routing decisions.

The results presented here motivates our further work toward the alternative solutions to realize inter-vehicular communication.

Chapter 4

UMTS and Peer-to-Peer

In the previous chapters we have listed a number of traffic efficiency application and argued why the current approaches to implement them in VANETs suffer from serious limitations. Undoubtedly, many of the proposed applications are highly useful and very desirable, but limited by market introduction and the technological hurdles of VANET-based solutions. What are the possible alternatives? Cheap mobile Internet access, be it via 3G, GPRS, WiMax, Wi-Fi, or any other technology is already widespread. UMTS flatrates, for instance, are available in many countries and are rapidly getting cheaper. Always-on mobile Internet access becomes reality now, long before VANET technology in cars will be deployed. In stark contrast to wireless multi-hop networks, the connectivity, latency, and bandwidth are almost independent from the physical distance between communicating parties when infrastructure-based communication is used. There are no separate network partitions, and differences in bandwidth or latency, if relevant at all, will only depend on the access technologies. In the first part of this chapter we will explain how a typical infrastructure-based communication network (UMTS) works and point out properties which are relevant for the development of a traffic information system.

The availability of a communication channel as offered by infrastructure-base networks does not automatically solve the problem of efficient data exchange between multiple users spread over a large geographical area. It rather constitutes a solid basis for such communication. Thus in the second part of this chapter we

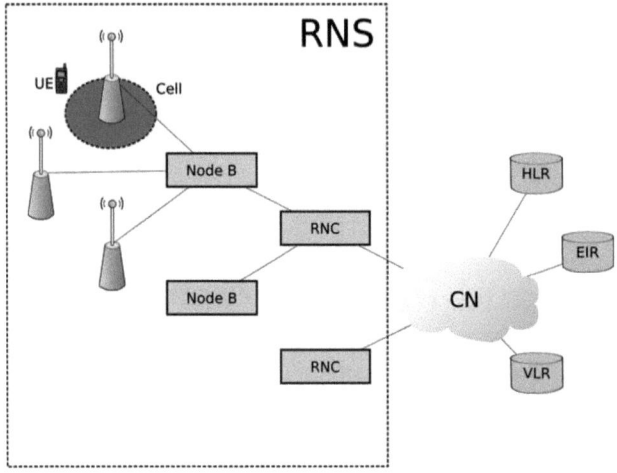

Figure 4.1: The architecture of the UMTS network.

will present the idea of overlay networks which facilitate efficient data exchange between the users.

4.1 Universal Mobile Telecommunications System (UMTS)

Probably the most popular infrastructure-based network offering service which is sufficient for our traffic information system is a UMTS network. Let us thus discuss the architecture and working principle of such a network in a more detailed manner (an overview of mobile communication systems can be found in [Sch03]). The Universal Mobile Telecommunications System (UMTS) is an example of a third generation mobile communication network, the successor of the second generation network: Global System for Mobile Communications (GSM). The names 2G and 3G networks are also commonly used. The process of specification of UMTS was overseen by the 3rd Generation Partnership Project (3GPP) [3gp].

The architecture of the UMTS network is depicted in Figure 4.1. It comprises of the Radio Network Subsystem (RNS) and the Core Network (CN). The whole radio network subsystem is also called UMTS Terrestrial Radio Access Network (UTRAN). The most important part of the RNS are Radio Network Controllers (RNC) which control one or many Node Bs. Each Node B can supervise several independent cells. User Equipment (UE) connects and communicates via the air interface within one cell at a time. There may be multiple users in one cell. As already stated, the most important part of the RNS are the RNC, which are responsible for: a) radio resource control, b) admission control, c) channel allocation, d) power control settings, e) handover control (between antennas or Node Bs), and f) ciphering of the messages. Node B, on the other hand, has to: a) control air interface by transmission and reception of the data, b) select appropriate modulation-demodulation algorithms, and c) detect and handle transmission errors.

The most popular UMTS air interface is W-CDMA (also called UTRA-FDD), which uses two 5 MHz bands at 2 GHz frequency, separately for up- and downlink. TD-CDMA (UTRA-TDD) is an alternative solution: it uses time division multiplex (rather than the expensive frequency multiplex) to separate up- and downlink of multiple users.

The Core Network Subset (CN) shares many elements with the 2G network (GSM/EDGE), which simplified the migration of existing GSM networks and reduced the financial burden for network operators. The Core Network brings the user data to their destination, and is therefore composed of a number of switching centers and gateways to other networks (like Internet or networks of other operators). The CN is divided into circuit switched (speech) and packet switched (data exchange) domains. Circuit switched elements include Mobile Switching Center (MSC), Home Location Register (HLR) (a database storing static information about users), Visitor Location Register (VLR) (storage with copies of the user data in a particular RNS and dynamic data, e. g., about the currently used network cell) and Equipment Identity Register (EIR) (a list of devices used in the network). A packet switched domain, that is a subsystem responsible for data exchange in the network, comprises of Serving GPRS Support Node (SGSN) and Gateway GPRS Support Node (GGSN). Some network elements, such as HLR, EIR and VLR, are shared by both domains.

Authentication is needed before use of the UMTS services. The authentication is crucial for billing purposes. Since one user can use multiple user equipments (i.e., mobile phones) so-called Subscriber Identity Modules (SIM) are used to decouple the user identity from the device he or she is currently using. Each SIM contains a Personal Identity Number (PIN), PIN Unblocking Key (PUK), authentication key (K_i) and International Mobile Subscriber Identity (IMSI). In the first step local authentication is required between the user and SIM to allow access to K_i; this is achieved when the user types in the correct PIN. In the next step authentication with the network operator is conducted. This is done with the help of the authentication key K_i and the UMTS MILENAGE algorithm. At its core MILENAGE uses the Advanced Encryption Standard (AES) algorithm. For authentication the network operator sends a random number (challenge) to the user. The random number is signed with K_i and the signed response (SRES) is sent back to the RNC. Since RNC possesses the same K_i (stored in the Authentication Center (AuC)), it is able to check the correctness of the SRES. After that Authentication and Key Agreement (AKA) takes place to establish a cipher key (CK), integrity key (IK) and authentication token (AUTN) used by the UE. The exchange of the data via the air interface is encrypted, thus confidentiality and integrity of the messages is ensured [WSA02]. User identity confidentiality is ensured by not using the permanent user identity (IMSI) on the radio link; instead, temporary identities are used. We will skip the details here, but UMTS also uses mutual authentication, which means that the mobile user and the serving network authenticate each other. In the original GSM design, it was possible to jeopardize user security by providing "false" base stations, because only authentication between the user and network (and not the other way around) was required.

From our perspective the most important services of the UMTS network are data exchange services. To establish a data connection in the UMTS network it is necessary to follow the steps defined by the Radio Resource Control Protocol (RRC) [Pro99]. UE sends a RRC Connection Request to its current RNC.

RNC can select appropriate Node B and answers the request with an RRC Connection Setup message. From this moment on further interactions with Serving GPRS Support Node (SGSN) are undertaken. In particular, they involve an authentication handshake in Radio Access Network Application Part Protocol (UMTS RANAP) [Ton99] between UE and SGSN. After this two parties agree on a session key, and further messages are exchanged with respective data about the requested connection, i. e., Direct Transfer Request and Response. A connection in the UMTS network is characterized by the so-called Packet Data Protocol (PDP) context, that is a set of settings that defines which networks may be used and the quality of service (bandwidth, latency, etc.) required by the application. The list of PDP contexts that a particular user is allowed to use is stored in the HLR. Afterward when the connection is established, an IP-based communication channel between UE and SGSN is created and remains active until the mobile station deactivates it. An application running on UE produces normal data packets which are sent via SGSN to the Internet (or in the case of two UE communicating with each other via Core Network). Note that similarly to data exchange in UTRAN, the communication between UE and SGSN (that is communication within the CN) is also encrypted.

Location management is a crucial functionality of the UMTS network. Whenever a network wants to set up a connection to a mobile station, the exact location area (that is UMTS cell) has to be known. It then pages the mobile station via the air interface. To make a mobile station aware of their location, the Node B broadcasts a specific, unique number called Location Area Index (LAI). When the number changes, the mobile station assumes the location changes and informs the Home Location Register about this fact. This principle allows for keeping the location data up-to-date with little effort. During an active connection the exact location (cell) of the UE is traced.

A UMTS network can provide users with an IP-based communication channel, that is exactly the same network protocol as used in the Internet. Although the functionality offered is the same, the quality of the service may differ. When using cellular 3G networks we can expect high data rates. The standard value offered nowadays is about 384 kbit/s, which is still inferior when compared to typical domestic Internet access realized via DSL. Therefore further effort was undertaken to increase both up- and downlink rates. This resulted in the definition of the High Speed Downlink Packet Access (HSDPA) and High-Speed Uplink Packet Access (HSUPA) standards which increased the bandwidth offered up to 21 Mbit/s. The successor of UMTS, the so-called Long Term Evolution (LTE) network, is already standardized and deployed on a small scale. It will offer even higher data rates of 50 Mbit/s [lte].

In contrast to VANET networks the communication between two UMTS users is not achieved via (re-)broadcast of the messages. Each user is connected with a UMTS antenna in his current cell. UMTS cells are separated from each other by using different frequencies, thus the transmission in one cell does not inhibit the communication in nearby cells. The data between cells are transmitted via the high-capacity Core Network. Also the cells of a different network provider in the same geographical area are separated from each other by using different frequencies.

As far as the network capacity of a single UMTS cell is considered, the results of experiments have shown that when using the 5 MHz carrier frequency, approximately 600–700 kbit/s cell capacity can be expected, while under perfect conditions values up to 2 Mbit/s were measured (single user, small interface) [WSA02]. A high number of users using small bit rates (rather than a small number of users using high bit rates) is favorable for a UMTS network. Experiments show that a single UMTS cell can handle up to 200 simultaneous users with constant bit rates of 20 kbit/s. When increasing the number of users the bandwidth drops to only about 10 kbit/s for 250 users [WSA02]. We should keep those values in mind when developing our infrastructure-based traffic information system.

Constant evolution of mobile Internet access networks like UMTS allows us to hope that the values presented will further improve in the future. Also the density and availability of the networks improves over time. An extreme example of this fact is the deployment of third generation communication network in the region covering the highest mountain of the world: Mount Everest [mou].

Our system will depend on infrastructure-based communication. The only assumption we are going to make is that there is an IP-based communication channel available for the users. In contrast to the aforementioned systems like TomTom HD Traffic we neither intend to change the way the network works nor demand access to special services or internal structures of the network (like HLR). Instead we adjust *our* system to work with the generic network as an ordinary mobile application running on UMTS.

4.2 Peer-to-Peer

The presence of an IP-based communication channel offered by an infrastructure-based network does not automatically allow for a successful deployment of a traffic information system. To establish a connection and exchange data with a remote station, the IP-address of this station has to be known. In our case it would mean that each user of our system would have to know the IP addresses of all the other participants; each measurement will then be sent to all the other users. Clearly such a solution is technically infeasible. Therefore we need to seek more efficient ways of exchanging data between multiple users of the system. In this thesis we will present a novel approach to implementing a car-to-car communication application upon infrastructure-base networks using peer-to-peer overlay networks. Overlay networks allow abstracting the underlying network protocol (like IP in our case) and facilitating direct sharing of the resources (storage, content, CPU cycles) between the users.

The decentralized nature inherent to VANETs is very appealing for traffic information systems. A cooperative approach in which each participant contributes, distributes, and consumes information, where no central institutions and no central infrastructure are necessary, and where, consequently, the absence of a single point of failure promises a robust service without recurring costs—all this is obviously highly desirable. In this work, we therefore look at an alternative means to implementing a cooperative TIS—*not* via VANETs with their severely limited information propagation speed and capacity, but *still* in a fully decentralized, self-organized, scalable, and cooperative fashion. Our technical basis of choice is a peer-to-peer overlay over mobile (cellular) Internet access.

Multiple definitions of the peer-to-peer can be found in the literature, for instance:

Definition (Peer-to-Peer Network). *Peer-to-Peer (P2P) are distributed systems consisting of interconnected nodes able to self-organize into networks with the purpose of sharing resources. Peers are usually equal in terms of functionality and tasks they perform [ATS04].*

The peer-to-peer paradigm has become quite popular recently, which can be attributed to the properties of P2P networks: they are scalable, fault-tolerant, and resistant to censorship and control [LCP+05]. Since they self-organize without the need of a central server the administration overhead is reduced. In this section we will provide the reader with a short introduction to the subject of peer-to-peer networks.

Successful applications of peer-to-peer networks can be divided into the following functional groups:

- communication and collaboration (instant messaging [jab], voice and video Internet telephony [sky]),
- distributed computation (SETI@home [seta]),
- distributed database systems [DHJ+07] or distributed file systems [KBC+00],
- content distribution: sharing digital media [RFH+01, SMLN+03], file-sharing [napb, gnu], publish/subscribe [EFGK03], streaming and application-level multicast [YLE04].

Traffic information systems are clearly systems sharing digital content (i. e., measurements), thus solutions from the last group presented above are applicable. Hybrid decentralized networks like Napster were the first attempt to realize distributed content sharing [napa, napb]. Each participant stored some content and a central server was used to maintain a list of all registered users (with connection data) and a list of files that each user wished to share in the network. A joining peer had to contact the server, announce its presence and the contents it wished to share. Requests for files were first sent to the server which returned a list of users that held some matching content. Afterward direct communication between the peers took place. The reasoning of the designers was simple: the actions producing a high network load (that is the actual distribution of content) were performed in a decentralized fashion, while the indexing, which is less costly, was carried out by a centralized server. As it turns out the scalability of the solution based on a central index was an issue and, even worse, the central index constituted the central point of failure, which rendered the system unusable.

The shortcomings of the first peer-to-peer network motivated further research towards fully-decentralized overlays. The design of a typical P2P network for content sharing includes a network of peers, connections between them and the distributed function of locating the content in the network. The structure of the peers can be pre-defined or created in a random fashion, thus such P2P networks are often divided into structured and unstructured.

One of the first fully decentralized overlay networks was for instance Gnutella [gnu]. In order to join Gnutella at least one peer which is already in the network has to be known (so-called bootstrapping peer). The joining process is initiated by sending a so-called *Ping* message to the bootstrapping peer. After the reception of a ping, the bootstrapping peer responds with a *Pong* message (acknowledging its current active status) and forwards the original message to some other peers in the network it is connected to. Each of those peers responds to the original peer with a pong. Hence the joining peer is able to establish a connection to other active peers. A set of connection data of other peers is called a routing table.

Each peer can share some content from its local storage to other peers. There is no particular data placement scheme in such networks. Thus in order to localize a particular piece of information usually brute force methods are employed. For instance the location of content in the original Gnutella was achieved by flooding:

a query message with a description of the searched content (e. g., a file name or file name wildcard) was sent to all known peers. Each of them first checked if it possessed content matching the request; if this was not the case, it passed the query to other peers it knew. If some matching content was found, the *Query Hit* message was sent back to the originator. To avoid loops in the network, each message had a unique ID (duplicates when detected were dropped). The header of the message contained a Time-to-Live (TTL) field which was decremented each time a message was forwarded. The usage of TTL allowed reducing the region of the network affected by forwarding the query. Setting the correct value was more a question of art than science: small values will not allow finding rare content which is present in the network but lies too far from the originator (in terms of overlay hops), whereas large values of TTL can lead to network overload. Although many improvements were proposed of the look-up process [LCC$^+$02, YGM02, ZJX07], the matter of fact is that in unstructured networks locating content involved many peers, in the worst case all of them (when searching for particularly rare content). The strengths of unstructured networks are their natural support of keyword searching and a usually high failure tolerance.

The researchers quickly noticed that graph theory can be successfully applied to analyze the properties of a peer-to-peer network. The set of connected peers can be abstractly described as a graph: each peer can be represented by a vertex and connections between the peers will be the edges of a graph. In a simplified sense a large part of the development in the peer-to-peer field was done by applying the following principle. In the first step a family of graphs was selected that possess some advantageous properties, e. g., a small diameter. Subsequently, protocols had to be developed to establish a peer structure similar to the selected graph in a self-organizing distributed manner. In contrast to the case of unstructured networks where the content was placed randomly in the network, here the data placement mechanism is pre-defined and known to all participants. When the content is placed at specific locations, the look-up can be realized more efficiently. There is a plethora of algorithms for efficient traversing of a graph. A family of peer-to-peer networks defining exactly how the peers should connect to each other and where the content should be put is called *structured networks*.

The most prominent example of structured peer-to-peer networks are Distributed Hash Tables (DHT). Similarly to its non-distributed counterpart, a DHT associates keys with values and offers a simple interface of distributed storage. The original idea of DHT was inspired by the works of Plaxton et al. [PRR97], where a scalable system was presented for accessing shared objects in a distributed environment. For this purpose a virtual balanced tree is created. A tree is a graph often used by efficient indexing structures. Each peer selects a random node u in this tree and connects to its parent and siblings in the tree. Furthermore, it is responsible for information associated with all nodes of the subtree rooted at u. Objects and nodes are identified in a semantic free fashion (for instance by bit fields). When searching for information the peer first checks if the information is located in its subtree (this is done by matching its ID and the ID of the object searched for). If this is not the case the look-up message is sent upwards in the tree structure (to its parent). Messages are routed by matching longer prefixes towards the peer responsible for the object. This scheme has a number of shortcomings. First and foremost the structure of the tree needs to be known in advance and cannot change over time. Hence the "capacity" of the tree cannot change and it is only possible to store as many distinct objects as there are nodes in the tree. Secondly, the hierarchical structure is not fault-resistant: a failure of a node placed high in the hierarchy makes the whole subtree of the original tree unavailable.

To address the former problem, Consistent Hashing [KLL$^+$97] can be applied. It was originally proposed in the context of web caching. The idea was to use standard hashing to place web objects across a network cache. Assuming the hashing method is widely known it can be used as an addressing scheme to locate proper objects in nearby caches. The hash function has a fixed and clearly defined range of possible values, in the peer-to-peer context, it can be used to generate trees for Plaxton-like routing which do not have to change over time and can be efficiently queried as explained above. On the other hand, the domain of a hash function is usually larger than its range, enabling efficient storage of a large set of key-value pairs.

A combination and extension of both ideas, i. e., Plaxton routing and Consistent

Hashing, forms the basis of almost all DHT algorithms proposed so far. The keys are then unambiguously mapped on so-called key space by means of consistent hashing. Similarly, peer IDs are also hashed on the key space. Each peer is thus responsible for a part of the key space and key in its direct vicinity. The main part of the DHT is the implementation of a *look-up* algorithm in a decentralized fashion. For a given key, the *look-up* returns the responsible peer. This is done in the following way. Participants form an overlay network, where each peer is connected to a number of "neighbors". Since the content is put in pre-defined locations (with the help of consistent hashing), some sort of greedy routing can be applied. In each step of the look-up process the message is sent closer and closer to its destination. For each intermediate peer the following applies: either a peer possesses a given key or it knows a peer offering progress towards the key searched for in the overlay. The exact way in which the peers are interconnected with each other depends on the system used, similarly different ways of generating key spaces are used. Let us now quickly review the most popular and widely cited examples of DHTs.

In Chord [SMLN+03] consistent hashing is achieved by SHA-1 hash function generating 160-bit length identifiers of objects and peers. The key space forms a ring. In Chord each peer maintains connections to $O(\log N)$ other peers and the location of data for a given key takes on average $(1/2)\log_2 N$ hops.

Since the management of data in a distributed fashion by way of a DHT is a complex, and yet critical, subject in the context of this thesis, we will describe it in a more detailed fashion by looking at a typical DHT. Figure 4.2 depicts a Chord ring with 128 possible identifiers (which is much less than in reality but makes the example comprehensible). In Chord both peers and keys are hashed to an identifier. These Chord-IDs form a ring structure. Each peer has a link to its direct successor (the peer with the next higher Chord-ID). The keys are also hashed and stored for their successors. In the example content identified by the name "File1" is hashed to Chord-ID 14. Thus the peer with Chord-ID 35 (successor of Chord-ID 14) is responsible for this key. Similarly the content identified by the name "File2" is stored by the peer with ID 2 (successor of 109 in the ring structure).

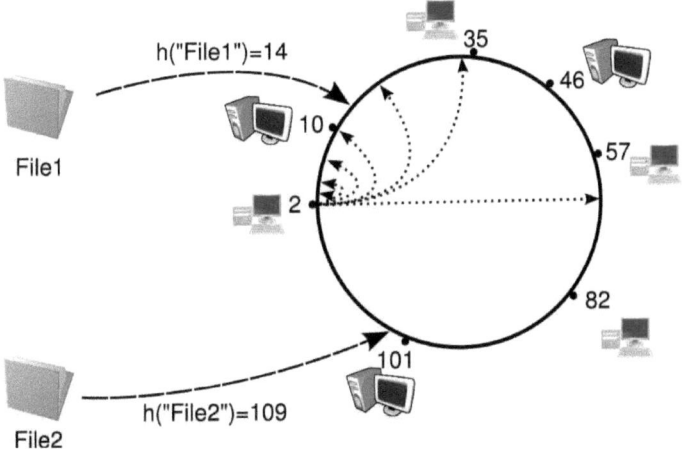

Figure 4.2: Distribution of data among peers in a Chord overlay network.

To find a peer responsible for a given key one has to send a *look-up* query along the ring. By passing it on to a neighbor it will reach its destination. For instance, in order to locate content of the "File1", the peer with the Chord-ID 2 would have to apply the hash function h on the string identifier "File1", and pass the look-up message with the destination address 14 to its direct successor (i.e. the peer with Chord-ID 10). The message will be sent along the ring until the peer responsible for the sector containing its destination address will be located; in our case this is the peer with the Chord-ID 35.

In order to perform queries more efficiently, each peer maintains a finger table with fingers pointing to peers that are at least 2^i IDs away with increasing i (depicted by the dotted lines). With this extension, the complexity of locating the responsible peer becomes logarithmic in the number of network participants. The look-up algorithm changes only slightly, by delivering messages a peer is selected which is closest to the destination address. This could be the direct successor or a more distant peer pointed by one of the fingers.

Peers can join and leave the network freely. Upon joining the new participant takes the responsibility for a given set of keys, reducing the average workload in the network. When leaving, the peer hands over the stored data to some other responsible peer. The random uniform allocation of the data and peers on the ring results in a fair load distribution, assuming all pieces of content are equally popular. To increase robustness of the system, redundant storage of the data can be introduced by using multiple hash functions. In this case each (key, value) pair is stored multiple times, usually by different peers.

The Content Addressable Network (CAN) [RFH+01] uses d-dimensional Cartesian coordinate space on a d-torus as the key space on which peers and keys are mapped. Each peer is responsible for a d-dimensional hypercube of the key space and is connected only to peers responsible for neighboring cubes, that is cubes with edges common to the original cube. Thus each peer has to maintain a routing table of size $O(d)$. The look-up is achieved by a greedy algorithm: a look-up message is passed to the cube closer to the key searched for. The complexity of this process is $O(d \cdot n^{1/d})$. When dimension of the CAN space is chosen as $d = \log N$ the complexity of the look-up and size of the routing table of CAN and Chord are equal.

Viceroy [MNR02] improves the design of the above-mentioned solutions. This is an example of a constant degree network: similar to CAN, the routing table size of a peer in this system is constant. Peers are organized into rings (levels) in the network. Upon joining, a peer selects a ring to join and connects to the predecessor and successor in this ring. Furthermore it also has connections to the higher and lower level peers and to so-called butterfly pointers ("left" and "right"). Despite the fact that the routing table is of constant size, the logarithmic complexity of the look-up can be achieved. The main shortcoming of this system is the quite complex structure that needs to be maintained. The system was developed under the assumption of the absence of peer failures, thus some researchers have pointed out that constant node degree can make the network partitioning more likely [LP02].

Quite a large number of peer-to-peer networks use de Bruijn graphs to build the peer structure. The reason for that is the very beneficial relation between the graph degree (size of a peer routing table) and the graph diameter (look-up complexity): for a given degree k, the diameter is $\log_k n$ (asymptotically). Examples of networks using de Bruijn graphs include Koorde [KK03], Cycloid [SXC06] and Distance Halving [NW03]. The properties of the Distance Halving network will be described as a representative of this group of peer-to-peer overlays. The key space is a continuous interval $I = [0,1)$ to which peers and data are hashed. In spite of constant node degree in this network, the routing complexity is only $O(\log n)$.

An important part of any working peer-to-peer system is the solution of the bootstrapping problem. Almost all systems presented so far assume that a peer which wishes to join the overlay network already knows at least one peer that is in the network. Since it is a common problem, a lot of solutions have been presented. Furthermore, the problem is somehow independent of the overlay used, and so are the solutions.

When implementing a working content sharing system using peer-to-peer, one can chose from among the following bootstrapping techniques. Gnutella used servers to bootstrap the overlay. A client had to resolve the DNS of a server name to get its IP address. Servers keep a list of addresses of the nodes in the overlay, while peers in the overlay send their contact information periodically to the servers so as to keep the bootstrapping list up to date.

The Domain Name System (DNS) is part of the standard Internet architecture, and can also be used directly to store contact data (e. g., IP addresses) of participating nodes without additional server architecture. For instance, such a solution was used in CAN.

As soon as a particular overlay protocol becomes very popular, a strategy of random address probing can be utilized to join the network. A peer wishing to join simply tries to connect to a random IP in the Internet. Provided a peer-to-peer client implementation uses well-known ports, it is possible to establish a connection with a peer which is already in the network. Of course the probability of successful detection depends on the popularity of the overlay. In [GG08], experiments on a brute-force random global scan for Gnutella peers revealed that on average 2425 attempts before finding the first peer inside Gnutella were required. The process can be accelerated by sophisticated algorithms for selecting a random IP to be probed. Due to the limitations of the random probing Gnutella also uses *host caches* for bootstrapping. Each peer maintains a list of nodes previously "seen" on the Gnutella network (for instance during the previous sessions). Join requests are sent to those peers as they may be still (or again) present in the overlay.

An interesting extension to the random probing mechanism allows using it also for less popular overlay protocols. It is possible to use a popular DHT to store bootstrapping information of a less popular network. For instance a list of nodes active in the target overlay can be maintained in a popular network (like Gnutella). A joining peer will first have to join Gnutella, then retrieve the list of currently active nodes, and bootstrap its connections in the other peer-to-peer network [CKF04].

If an Internet access technology allows it, local flooding can be used to obtain contact data of a bootstrapping node. In Local Area Networks (LAN) built upon Ethernet, it is possible to sent broadcast packets which will be delivered to all computers using the same LAN. This method is similar to random probing; however reaching all nodes in a local domain is achieved with one "probing".

4.3 Conclusion

In this chapter we presented important prerequisites to our novel peer-to-peer based traffic information system. In particular, we have explained the working principle of a cellular, infrastructure-based communication network on the example of UMTS and its advantages over VANETs as far as the exchange of data between multiple users spread over a large area is concerned. Subsequently the basic idea of peer-to-peer networks was presented, together with a short review of related work dealing with the subject. A peer-to-peer overlay is built upon existing infrastructure-based communication networks, and is therefore able to preserve its positive properties. The use of peer-to-peer allows for an efficient implementation of large systems to share digital content.

Among the subjects discussed in a peer-to-peer community, range queries are probably the closest to what is needed to implement a cooperative traffic information system in a distributed manner. We show their inapplicability in Appendix B.

Using infrastructure-based communication naturally also yields the possibility of a centralized system, like the one discussed in [SSC$^+$10], with all the well-known advantages and drawbacks of such an approach. Compared to a peer-to-peer solution, a centralized system poses different technical challenges which we described in [LRSM08]. We argue that a distributed approach is preferable if it is able to deliver the same service in comparable quality—not least because it avoids the effort in setting up and maintaining the central components. There may also be a less technical reason why peer-to-peer sharing of cooperatively gathered traffic information is more appropriate than a server-based solution: the latter implies that a single authority may determine who may use the data. Given that this data are collected by the users themselves and given that access to this data is important to the society as a whole, this does not seem to be appropriate. We believe that traffic data should be freely accessible by anyone wishing to participate in a distributed traffic information system.

Chapter 5

A Peer-to-Peer Structure for Traffic Information Systems

The idea of communicating cars has gained a lot of attention over the recent years. *Traffic Information Systems* (TIS), the subject of this thesis, are a particularly popular representative of car-to-car applications. The main goal of these applications is to provide each car with information on the current traffic situation along its planned route. A navigation system may use this data to determine better routes adapted to the current dynamics of road traffic or unexpected circumstances like accidents.

As we already explained, when such systems are realized using VANETs, they will necessarily suffer from the inherent limitations of wireless ad-hoc networks, i.e., limited network capacity and limited connectivity. It will also take a significant amount of time until the necessary market penetration of VANET technology is achieved. In order to avoid these limitations, here we consider an *alternative* way of realizing such a system. Instead of using VANET technology, we will rely on infrastructure-based cellular communication, such as for example UMTS.

Peer-to-peer overlay networks offer robust and efficient search and retrieval of data along with redundant storage and massive scalability [LCP+05]. Therefore, a peer-to-peer overlay over cellular networks constitutes a point in the design space that offers very interesting opportunities: it exhibits the robustness and decentrality properties of a VANET-based system, but it avoids the scalability and connectivity issues of VANETs.

In this chapter we first take a closer look at the application and discuss the proposed overlay structure. To underpin our argumentation we shall start with a naive approach to using generic DHT for storing traffic related data. Based on this example we will point out the unique characteristics of the TIS application and customize the DHT to account for these characteristics. We call our customized system *PeerTIS*. The evaluation of the proposed solution with regard to bandwidth usage, overall performance and scalability will conclude the chapter.

5.1 The TIS application

5.1.1 Framework and use case

As already explained, a cooperative TIS is essentially a set of shared traffic-related information, along with mechanisms to access, use, and update it. In our case the shared information consists of travel times along road segments. We assume that all participants are equipped with a GPS receiver, a digital map, and mobile Internet access. All this can be provided by state-of-the-art cell phones, but other platforms are equally conceivable. The digital maps are used as a basis for addressing road segments, so that each road segment can be assigned a unique ID that is known to every participant. In the following, we thus use "key" and "road segment" interchangeably. The combination of GPS and map data allows each car to determine the ID of the road segment it is currently traveling on, and the IDs of the road segments it intends to pass along its future route. An observation of the current travel time consequently consists of a timestamp, a road segment ID, and the measured travel time.

Usually, a car's navigation system will fetch the relevant data at the beginning of the journey. This includes measurements describing the current situation along the possible routes connecting the origin and the intended destination.

A requesting peer is provided with a record that describes the current traffic condition on the queried road segment. This record is generated upon request by the peer that is responsible for the road segment, based on the information that has previously been uploaded by other participants. It could, for instance, characterize the average driving speed reported in the recent past.

5.1.2 Tackling a TIS with P2P techniques

At a first glance, the problem is amazingly simple: the data stored in the traffic information system possess natural addressing identifiers: street segment IDs. Therefore, we can use the segment IDs as keys and the available measurements on the segment as values. So, *in principle*, we could use any of the plethora of existing DHTs, and simply apply it to TIS data. However, we can do much better if we keep the specifics of the application in mind.

It actually turns out that the implementation of a traffic information system using a peer-to-peer overlay over cellular Internet access is far from straightforward in several regards. First, mobile devices and cellular Internet access themselves pose challenges. Despite the rapid development of infrastructure-based cellular networks, the offered service (in terms of bandwidth and latency) is still inferior in comparison to, for instance, domestic Internet access. Moreover, typical on-board devices are usually equipped with less storage and weaker CPUs. In order to deal with the limited resources of the mobile stations, the reduction of the communication burden in the overlay is necessarily a primary design goal. So far, this goal is obviously common to most peer-to-peer overlays. However, here, the considered application itself provides very interesting opportunities to achieve them—opportunities that are not present in the context of distributed hash tables in general.

This is because, beyond the challenges of the technological platform, a quite unique feature of a TIS is the very specific usage pattern. As noted above, a navigation system will typically fetch all the data relevant for the planned and alternative routes, and will refresh the necessary information periodically. It will also contribute a measurement whenever a road segment has been passed. First, we observe that the look-ups at the beginning and upon refresh operations have a very bursty structure: in most cases, many road segments will be looked up at once. Furthermore—and this is the key point—there is an inherent structure in the accessed data elements: they are not random access operations to independent keys, as they are typically assumed (implicitly or explicitly) when DHTs are designed and analyzed. Instead, the usage pattern has interesting *locality properties*: Since information about long, contiguous routes through the road network is required, a car will issue requests about many segments that are geographically close together. Moreover, if a car contributes its observations for a road segment, it will typically have requested information about this road segment at an earlier time—it will usually only pass road segments that lie on its planned route. We show in our work how these interrelations between the user's actions can be used to improve the performance of our system.

5.2 A P2P overlay for traffic information systems

In this section, we explain the details of our realization of a peer-to-peer overlay based traffic information system, called PeerTIS. The main question to be answered in this context is: what kind of overlay structure is able to provide efficient means for storing and retrieving highly dynamic traffic information in a mobile environment, taking the previously discussed locality of requests and updates into account? As it turns out, the locality property shifts some tradeoffs in a direction that is very different from what is commonly discussed in the context of peer-to-peer overlays.

We will start this section with a naive approach: we simply use an existing, well-known DHT, the Content Addressable Network (CAN) by Ratnasamy et al. [RFH+01]. We will then, step by step, point out how it is possible to substantially improve on that, until, finally, we will arrive at the full PeerTIS design.

5.2.1 Naive approach

The Content Addressable Network (which we have already mentioned in Chapter 4) was one of the very first DHTs proposed. The keys stored in CAN are mapped to points in a d-dimensional space by a pre-defined hash function. The key space is divided into zones, one zone per peer, so that each point in the key space is assigned to one zone and therefore also to a peer. Each peer is responsible for storing the information assigned to all keys that fall into its zone. When a new peer joins, the zone of one existing peer is split in half, the new peer takes over one half, including the corresponding (key,value)-pairs. When peers leave, zones are merged and respective data are handed over. Further mechanisms exist to react in case of peer failures and other adversarial events.

The communication overlay is formed by connecting the peers that share a common edge between their zones in the key space. Each node maintains a small routing table containing the IP addresses and ports of peers responsible for the neighboring zones. Store and look-up operations can then be routed through the overlay by greedily forwarding them in the "direction" of their destination in the key space: a peer that performs a look-up checks in its routing table which neighbor offers the most progress in the key space towards the hashed coordinates and passes the look-up message to that neighbor. This peer is either responsible for the zone containing the sought-after key, or it forwards the request to one of its neighbors offering further progress towards the destination in the key space. This greedy forwarding continues until the message eventually reaches the peer responsible for the zone containing the point. For a much more in-depth description of the CAN overlay, we refer the reader to [RFH+01].

In a naive application of CAN to a cooperative traffic information system, one might proceed as follows. In order to access the data for route planning, a participating car will first identify the IDs of the relevant road segments. It will then use the hash function to determine the position of these IDs in the key space, and locate the peers responsible for these segments—one after the other. Note that due to the hashing of the keys, the positions of distinct road segment IDs in the ID space are entirely independent.

The process of accessing the data is depicted in Figure 5.1. This figure shows an example road and a (two-dimensional) CAN key space, that is subdivided into 18 zones (corresponding to 18 cars currently participating in the system). The dashed arrows show how the segments of a single road are mapped into the structure. The long solid arrow indicates that the car shown in the figure is responsible for the top-left zone in the CAN key space. Note that this has nothing to do with the physical position of the car: the responsibility zone is assigned randomly when the car joins the overlay (i.e., when the navigation device is switched on), and may later be adjusted through splitting and merging as other peers join and leave. It does not, however, relate to the position or movement of the car itself. By doing so we can almost neglect the movement of the cars: in contrast to VANET-based communication, UMTS-like communication is almost independent from the distance between the communicating parties. If the car intends to look up the currently available information about the three road segments ahead of it, it needs to generate three separate look-up requests which will follow the CAN overlay paths as indicated by the solid black arrows.

5.2.2 Improving the look-up performance

In many peer-to-peer applications (e.g., file sharing systems), queries are largely independent from each other. As pointed out above, in a traffic information system, in contrast, they are *not* independent. The key reason is the inherent structure of the stored data, resulting from the road segment neighborhood relation in the road network. In the naive approach outlined above, however, this structure is lost due to hashing. We therefore propose to keep the adjacent segments of the streets "close" to each other in the peer-to-peer structure. In other words, we aim to preserve the structure of the street network within the overlay network.

This aim can be achieved by leaving out hashing altogether. We may leave the general structure of the CAN overlay as it is, but instead of hashing road segment IDs to d-dimensional coordinates in an artificial coordinate space, we use a two-dimensional space, and use the *geographical coordinates* of each road

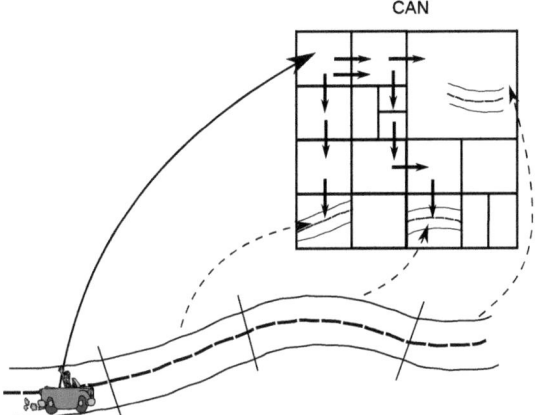

Figure 5.1: Naive application of CAN to a TIS. Dashed arrows show how the road segments are mapped into the structure. Bold solid arrows indicate the hops in the overlay necessary, for the peer in the left top zone, to fetch the data.

segment in the real world as key coordinates. In such a system, the peers are no longer responsible for zones in a virtual multi-dimensional key space, but for geographical areas and the traffic measurements that fall within these areas.

By doing so, we may reasonably expect to reduce the total effort that is necessary when a burst of look-ups for all road segments along one or more alternative routes occurs: the requested road segments are contiguous in the road network, neighboring segments are geographically close together. Consequently, if their location in the CAN space corresponds to the position in the real world, they will be managed by peers that are close together in the overlay structure. Therefore, much more efficient look-ups become possible. To retrieve the information on a whole route, it is then sufficient to locate the peer responsible for *one* particular segment of this route, and then to simply follow the route in the peer-to-peer overlay. One single "multi-hop look-up", forwarded along the requested route in the overlay, can collect all the required data.

To underpin our design principle, we have analyzed the query behavior of a cooperative traffic information system in a simulation of a full, real-city road network. For this purpose we used a road traffic simulator called SUMO [KHRW02] to generate car movements on a real street map of the German city of Düsseldorf, extracted from the OpenStreetMap project [OSM]. A more detailed description of our simulation setup follows in Section 5.3. We have analyzed the routes taken by the participating cars and found out that, on average, the routes incorporated more than 70 segments. Thus it can be expected that a car will be interested in more than 70 distinct, yet contiguous road segments, and presumably even more while dynamic routing will generate requests for alternative routes as well. Correlated, non-independent key look-ups for adjacent, consecutive road segments thus clearly dominate the request traffic of the application.

The look-up messages in our modified overlay differ from the ones used by the original CAN in an important aspect: they contain not just one single key to be looked up, but a whole sequence of road segments for which information is requested. Because the peers in CAN are connected to their direct neighbors, the process of "following" can take place without further look-ups by simply handing the request over from peer to peer. Each peer forwarding a request will simply provide the information it is responsible for, before passing the request further on to the next peer. This is a substantial benefit over the situation in the naive approach, where individual and independent look-ups were necessary to many independent positions scattered throughout the overlay.

In Figure 5.2, we show what would happen in the same example as in Figure 5.1 above. The desired information can now be easily accessed using *one* multi-hop look-up, causing significantly less communication overhead in the network

We will demonstrate that the complexity of one individual road segment look-up has, in fact, at most a marginal influence on the overall system performance: whether the employed peer-to-peer overlay can look-up the initial segment of a query in, for instance, $O(\sqrt{n})$ (like two-dimensional CAN) or $O(\log n)$ (like, e. g., Chord [SMLN+03]) steps barely matters—but at the same time it is absolutely

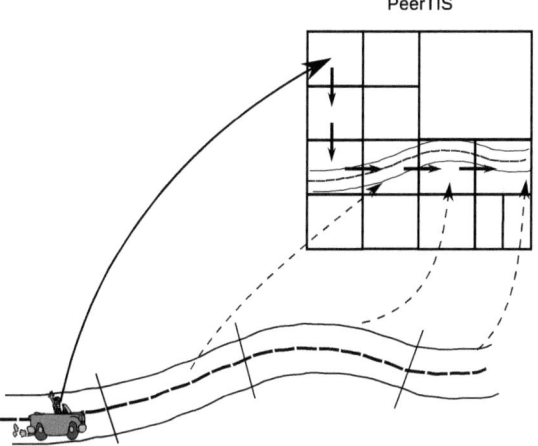

Figure 5.2: Preservation of the road network structure in the PeerTIS overlay.

vital how well it can handle correlated queries for larger groups of consecutive road segments.

5.2.3 Load distribution

The substitution of hash coordinates with geographical ones allows, as noted above, to save significant effort when peers issue bursts of look-ups for consecutive groups of road segments. However, it comes at a costs of its own: in contrast to *de facto* random hash coordinates, the geographical coordinates of road segments are not uniformly distributed over the key space. This has implications for the load distribution and fairness in the overlay. For instance, peers responsible for a zone in the city center, with many roads and lots of traffic, will experience a higher load than peers that manage a rural area.

We propose to tackle this problem by adjusting the zone sizes. In the original CAN, a joining peer would pick a random position and locate the peer currently responsible for this position. This zone would then be split, with the new peer taking over one half of it. Because larger zones are more likely to be "hit" than smaller ones by a newly joining peer, this results in relatively homogeneous zone sizes. This is acceptable when keys are uniformly distributed over the key space. In our case, we must accept a less uniform key distribution, because we want to preserve the locality relations between road segments in the overlay. Therefore, we apply a modification that leads to smaller zone sizes in areas with more data. Referring to the example above, the subdivision into zones should be much finer in the city center than in the rural area. As a consequence, the workload imbalance is reduced. However, we still neglect the movement of the peers. Accounting for the changing position of a peer would needlessly increase the maintenance overhead of the peer-to-peer structure.

A better load distribution can be achieved by taking into account the physical position of cars at the time when they join the network. Instead of joining at a random position in the key space, peers join in the area containing their *own current location*. This is easily possible with PeerTIS because it natively supports geographical addressing, meaning that the zone containing the geographical positions can be found with look-up messages as explained earlier. Consequently, there will be more peers joining in areas with a higher density of vehicles and data, and fewer in the "unpopular" ones.[1]

A very beneficial side-effect of these *geographical joins (Geojoins)* is a further improvement in the look-up performance. In most cases, directly after joining the network, the new peer will fetch all the data needed to make its routing decision. Since the planned route will start at the current position of a car, and the new peer joined in the overlay at least near to this position, the number of hops needed for the first look-up will be very small. As an illustration, the reader can refer back to Figure 5.2, and imagine that the initial look-up is made not from the top left zone but directly from the zone containing the first segment of the queried route.

---

[1] It should be noted here that the original hash-based CAN, just like any other DHT, also suffers from unbalanced load: the uniform distribution of keys does not necessary guarantee a uniform distribution of workload, since some keys (so-called "hot spots") are more popular than others.

5.2.4 Exploiting temporal correlations

Besides the *structural* dependencies between the queries that we have used above to improve the performance of bursts of look-ups for geographically connected road segments, there are also *temporal* correlations between the users' actions. In particular, subsequent requests and updates by the same peer are very likely to refer to the same geographic area, or even to the same road segments. When, while driving, the information on the planned route is refreshed, a very similar set of road segments will be looked up. Furthermore, when a car produces its own traffic measurements, this will typically happen for segments on its route—i.e., for segments which it has requested previously.

This peculiarity opens interesting avenues for further improvements. We suggest that each peer should maintain, apart from the standard routing table, a cache of contact data to peers that are responsible for the road segments on its planned route. This cache can be used to improve both the periodical update requests and the upload of measurements. It is quite likely that the same peers will be responsible for the data. Using the information from the cache, they can be contacted without any new look-up traffic.

Due to the limited resources of the mobile devices, it is highly desirable to avoid excessive node state. However, the cached information comes at a very small cost: it is a side-effect of the previous look-ups, and, apart from a few kilobytes of memory for storing the cache, it does not require any additional effort for maintenance. Of course, lack of active maintenance of the cached information means that it may be outdated when it is used later on.

But even if the cached information is not perfectly up to date, it may be helpful: even if the peer previously responsible for a given segment has meanwhile accepted a join request and handed over the data to a new peer, it will still be very "close" to the desired information. It will therefore be able to pass the request on to the correct peer with very little effort. So, once again, we take advantage of preserving the inherent structure of the data in the overlay.

If a cached entry happens to be completely invalid—for instance, when the peer has meanwhile left the network—there remains the option of conducting a regular look-up in the overlay. As a result, in this case, nothing is lost.

5.3 Evaluation

In the previous section, we have shown how PeerTIS is an adaptation of CAN to the very specific structure of traffic data. We will now evaluate this approach, using a prototype implementation of the system in a simulation framework. This includes an estimation of the bandwidth usage, as well as the expected latency and the quality of the provided information.

5.3.1 Simulation setup

We implemented the proposed algorithms and protocols in the peer-to-peer simulator OverSim [BHK07], which we coupled with a road traffic simulator called SUMO [KHRW02]. The latter was responsible for generating car movements on a real street map of the city of Düsseldorf, extracted from the OpenStreetMap project [OSM]. There were up to about 5 000 simulated vehicles underway in this city. Our main motivation for using a fully-fledged road traffic simulator like SUMO was to obtain realistic query and update patterns, which are vital for testing the applicability of the modified overlay structure for real-world implementations.

Cars in SUMO were coupled with OverSim peers. In our simulations we assumed that only about 20 % of cars participated in the system. Hence there were about 1 000 peers in the overlay and more cars on the streets. When a participating car set off on its journey we created a new peer; upon arrival at its destination the peer left the overlay. We usually simulated 2 000 seconds of road traffic for each simulation run. During that time we encountered substantial churn: ca. 30 % of the peers left the network and were replaced by a similar number of new ones.

The communication between the peers was realized in OverSim (via the underlying network simulator OMNeT++ [OMN]). The two main interactions between peers were the periodic retrieval of information regarding current traffic conditions and publishing of the measurements. To increase the reality degree of the information retrieval we implemented dynamic routing on peers. Upon creation the peers selected $a = 3$ possible alternative routes to their destination with the help of modified Dijkstra's Algorithm [CMM95]. Then the description of the routes was requested from the system and the fastest one with regard to the current traffic conditions was selected and the car set off. Each time a car had traversed a road segment it contributed the measurement of its travel time along that segment. In order to keep in touch with the current traffic situation, peers performed periodic reassessments of their routes once every three minutes. This was done by again calculating possible alternatives, requesting the data and possibly adjusting the route. Chapter 7 will be devoted to the particular subject of dynamic routing.

Each participant maintained a small storage with the measurements describing the street segments in its responsibility. Upon joins or leaves the data were handed over as described earlier.

At the beginning of the simulation, all initially present cars will join the overlay almost at the same time. Such a situation will obviously not occur in the real world, where cars join and leave continuously. We therefore removed the initial seconds of simulation time from our evaluations, giving the system time to reach a stable state. A stable state does not mean that the set of participating peers is constant, but rather that the overall number of peers remains more or less the same: new peers join the network and others leave the network as soon as they reach the planned destination. The overhead caused by these changes in the structure of the overlay is of course included in the evaluation.

5.3.2 Feasibility

In the first part of the evaluation, we concentrate on the feasibility of the proposed system in terms of bandwidth and latency demands. Figure 5.3 shows the average bandwidth usage. For each simulation second, we sum up the sizes of all transmitted messages. We differentiate between the maintenance overhead for the peer-to-peer structure (like periodic keep alive messages) and the traffic caused by traffic information application (the insertion of new data and queries). The figure shows the mean value from 3 independent simulation runs, for all active users along with 95 % confidence intervals. The values are very small (note that the y-axis is bytes/s, not kB/s). They easily fit the theoretical bounds of the UMTS networks (384 kbit/s for upload). Older cellular systems, like EDGE or GSM/GPRS, would likewise be able to handle such traffic amounts. The values obtained in field tests (see e. g., [WSA02, WCML07]) suggest that a throughput of ca. 40 kB/s between mobile nodes is feasible with UMTS. We compare the naive application of the original CAN overlay as described in Section 5.2.1 to our modified overlay, PeerTIS. As expected due to the reduced number of hops in look-up processing, PeerTIS causes a substantially lower bandwidth consumption despite the fact that the overlay maintenance overhead is the same for both overlays (the lines are indistinguishable on the plot).

To assess the scalability of the system, we tested it in simulations with increasing penetration ratios. As can be seen in Figure 5.4, the impact of varying penetration ratios on the average bandwidth usage per peer is negligible. This is a result of the self-scalability of the peer-to-peer system: on the one hand, each new peer increases the total load in the system, but on the other hand it compensates for this by also contributing resources to the system.

Although the average values of bandwidth usage are much smaller than the bandwidth offered by typical mobile Internet access, it may still happen that the network is locally overloaded by many peers concentrated in one cell of the cellular network. Thus, we determined another set of values in order to look at the load per UMTS cell. However, an approximation was employed since neither information on the positions of UMTS base stations nor on the

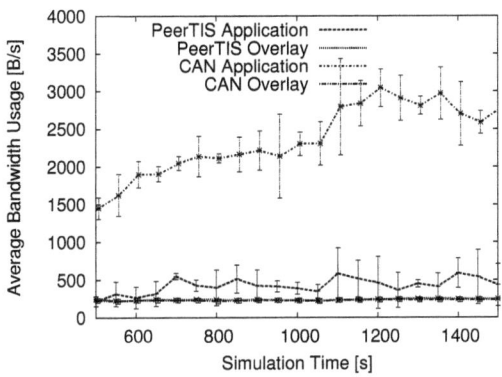

Figure 5.3: Average peer bandwidth usage.

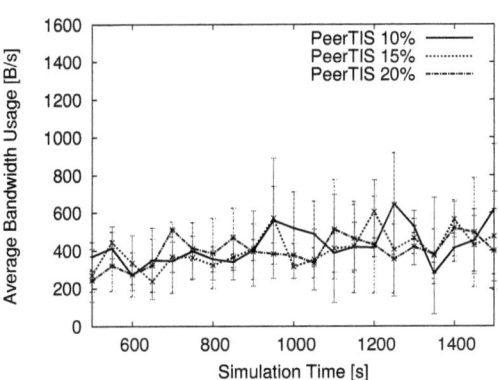

Figure 5.4: Scalability: Average peer bandwidth usage.

shapes of the respective cells were available to us. We divided the scenario into a grid of square cells, sized 500×500 m each, and measured the total amount of traffic transferred in each cell during an interval of five seconds length in the middle of the simulation. The snapshot of the network load is visualized as a heatmap in Figure 5.5, which shows the load of each cell in the simulation area. The distribution of the load reflects the topology of the city we used for the simulation. Clearly the load caused in the city center is higher than in the suburbs. The values obtained for the cells with the highest load added up to about 15 kB over five seconds, suggesting that the local network overload is not a problem. One may expect an even better situation in the real world if the load is divided between multiple service providers—our system does not assume at any point that all navigation systems communicate using the same service provider.

We have also estimated the number of simultaneous connections in each cell in a given time interval; the values of up to 90 connections can also be easily handled by cellular mobile access networks. They can serve up to 200 users with constant bit rates of 20 kbit/s. When the number of users is increased the bandwidth drops down (only about 10 kbit/s for 250 users) [WSA02]. These results show that even when the traffic information system application cannot use the UMTS network exclusively but rather shares the bandwidth with other applications, the induced load remains within safe values that can be handled by a network.

As expected, the non-hashing peer-to-peer overlay is susceptible to an unbalanced load distribution. Figure 5.6 shows the cumulative distribution of storage load on the peers. After 1 800 seconds of simulation we generate a snapshot of the storage content maintained by each peer in the network. The figure presents a number of segments (keys) for which data are available. From the figure it becomes clear that 40 % of the participants do not store any data. The countermeasure proposed in Section 5.2.3 (geographical joins) offers here a significant improvement. However, a hash-based DHT (original CAN in this case) remains superior with respect to fair load distribution.

An unbalance can also be observed in the bandwidth usage of single peers. We

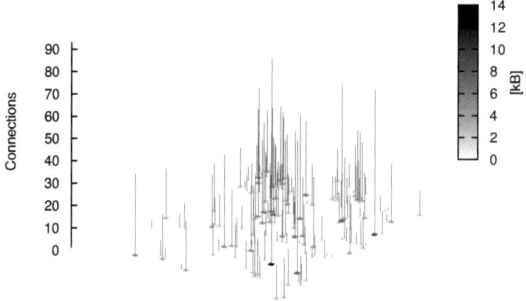

Figure 5.5: Per-cell network usage in 5 s time slots.

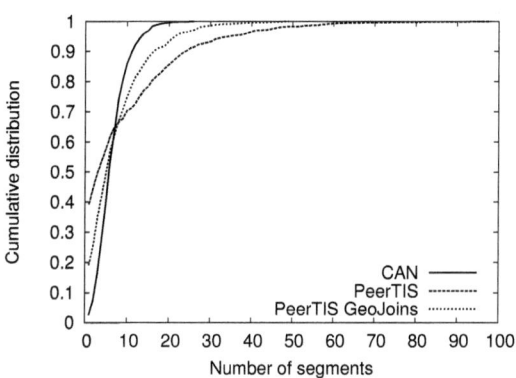

Figure 5.6: Load distribution in the network.

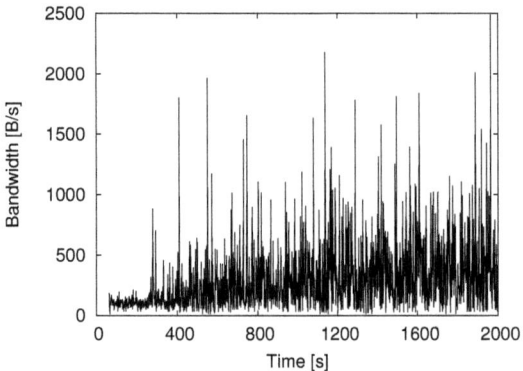

Figure 5.7: Bandwidth usage history of the busiest peers.

identified the busiest peers by adding the sizes of all packets sent and received over the whole time span of a car's participation in the network. The bandwidth usage history of this peer is presented in Figure 5.7. The busiest peer was in the unlucky position of receiving a sequence of joins (splitting its area few times), causing significant peaks in its bandwidth usage history. Recall that each such split (or merge) includes a hand-over of the data stored in the affected zone. Although the values are higher than the average presented above—up to 2.5 kB/s—they are still perfectly feasible with a GPRS or UMTS mobile Internet connection. Hence, we may conclude that despite the imperfectly balanced load distribution, no peer has to spend an excessive amount of resources.

5.3.3 Performance

The results presented above show that, from a technical point of view, the proposed system is feasible. From a practical perspective, however, it is important to see if it can provide a quality of service that matches the demands of the end users. In the context of this question, we analyzed the average response time of the system. Since the responses for the queries are exchanged directly between

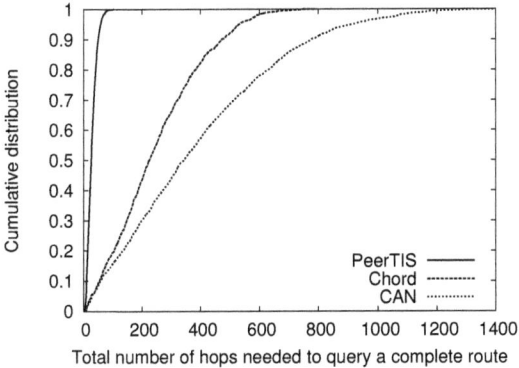

Figure 5.8: Total number of hops needed to query a complete route.

the peers, the most important factor influencing the response time is the number of hops in the overlay. Figure 5.8 shows the cumulative distribution function of the hop counts. The advantages of preserving the structure of the data stored can be seen clearly. Our system by far outperforms typical DHTs like CAN or Chord, despite the $O(\log n)$ look-up complexity for random keys offered by the latter overlay.

The number of hops in the overlay can easily be translated into latency times by multiplying the number of hops by the measured real UMTS latency. In real world experiments, a latency of about 450 ms has been measured for two mobile nodes using an UMTS network [WCML07] (with no HSDPA or HSUPA).

The look-up can be further speed up by caching the results of previous look-ups. In order to assess the influence of such caching we examined the number of hops which are needed to reach the first segment of the query. The results are depicted in Figure 5.9. It turns out that the proposed adjustments of the peer-to-peer structure result in a situation where almost 70 % of all queries need only one hop (they are sent directly) to reach the peer responsible for the first segments of the look-up. Both mechanisms proposed for achieving shorter look-up paths in the overlay—preserving the structure of the road network and caching

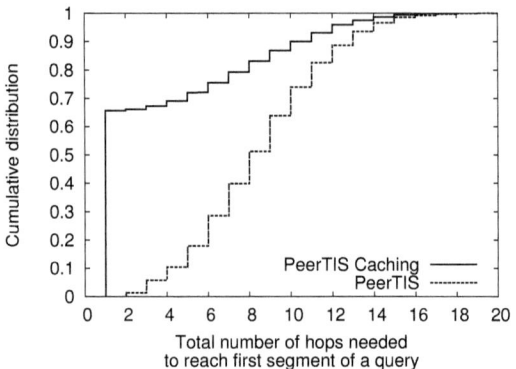

Figure 5.9: Effects of contact caching in PeerTIS.

contact data to responsible peers—can play very well together. It is worth noting that caching contact data can also be used in the unmodified CAN or Chord overlay, assuming the presence of correlations between subsequent user actions. Nevertheless, caching only shows its full potential in combination with the non-hashed, structure-preserving PeerTIS overlay.

5.4 Conclusion

In this chapter we presented PeerTIS, a dynamic, cooperative traffic information system using an Internet-based peer-to-peer overlay. Existing mobile Internet access technology is used as its foundation. This is combined with a peer-to-peer overlay tailored to the specific properties of the application: spatial and temporal correlations between users' actions, structural dependencies among the data that are stored in the system, and awareness of the current user position.

We have performed simulations on the basis of a prototype implementation. The results underline the feasibility of such a system. They also show that a large reduction of required bandwidth at the peers and an even more significant reduction of the necessary number of hops per look-up can be achieved by tailoring the overlay structure to the specific properties of the application.

Chapter 6

Graph-based Peer-to-Peer Structure

The evaluations from the previous chapter show that substituting hashed IDs with geographical coordinates in a generic DHT CAN yields considerable performance improvements as far as the retrieval and storage of traffic information are considered. There are, however, some blemishes on this facade. The reason why classical peer-to-peer algorithms (like CAN or Chord) use hashing for data placement is that it distributes the data evenly over the key space. In contrast to the *de facto* random hash coordinates, the geographical coordinates of road segments are not uniformly distributed over the key space. As we have shown it has some negative ramifications for the load distribution and fairness in the overlay. A proposed modification in the form of Geojoins bring some improvement but as we show it has some limitations. Therefore in this chapter we now consider an alternative means to distribute the data to the peers which deviates from classical DHT designs as far as the data placement algorithms are considered.

6.1 A street graph-based approach

In the previous chapter we discussed the use of an adjusted DHT for storing traffic related data in an efficient fashion. The solution has however a significant drawback in that leaving out hashing caused an unfair load distribution. For instance, peers that are responsible for a zone in a city center, with many roads

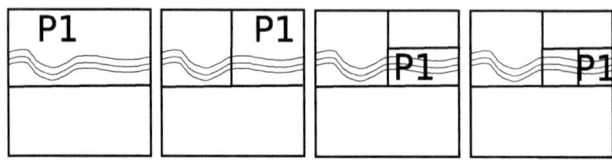

Figure 6.1: Sequence of joins in one region of overlay in PeerTIS.

and a lot of traffic, might experience a much higher load than peers that manage a rural area of the same size. In the extreme case, a peer will be responsible for a zone without any roads (located, for instance, in a park, an agricultural area, etc.).

Although Geojoins allow mitigating the problem, they have limitations. Let us look at an example of a sequence of joins in one region of a PeerTIS overlay, as depicted in Figure 6.1. Peer **P1** responsible for a zone with a street accepts 3 subsequent joins. Notice that not every join reduces the load of the original peer: some of them produce empty zones in the structure, that is zones that will *never* contain any data. Geojoins can amplify this unpleasant effect of the emergence of empty zones. Apart from an unfair workload distribution, such empty zones may even worsen look-up performance, as queries routed through them must pass the respective peers and thus experience increased latency.

Unfair load distribution undermines the whole principle of peers cooperating in the peer-to-peer structure with all participants having equal rights and obligations. Clearly, the way the key space (and consequently the data) is distributed between the peers does not yet fit the specific requirements of a traffic information system very well.

We now consider an alternative means of distributing data to the peers which deviates from classical DHT designs. A central characteristic of our application is that the full key space and its structure are known to all the peers: each peer has a local copy of the street map, and thus knows all the road segments, their IDs, and how they are connected to each other. The road network graph thus provides a clear structure for the key space and characterizes the interdependencies between the keys. This type of detailed knowledge about existing keys and their interrelation does not necessarily exist in other peer-to-peer applications. We will make use of this property to design an entirely different and innovative way of distributing data to peers. We call this system *GraphTIS*.

The GraphTIS design builds directly upon the road network graph. We depart from the concept of using geographic coordinates. Instead, we partition the road network graph into disjoint subgraphs, and assign each overlay node to one of these subgraphs. The peers are interlinked to form an overlay. Partitioning the road network graph instead of the geographic coordinate space gives us a lot of flexibility. In particular, there will be no empty or "near-empty" zones because each peer is assigned a subgraph of approximately equal size, and thus potentially all participants store some data. Areas without streets will simply not be present in the street graph.

To achieve that we have to employ graph partitioning algorithms which are able to dissect the graph into a number of (almost) equally-sized disjoint subgraphs. Our aim, of course, is still to minimize the effort involved in looking up a group of road segments. Whenever a query crosses a boundary between two peers, it must be transmitted over the network, causing network traffic and increasing the query latency. Thus, the partitions should be formed and interlinked in such a way that typical queries "touch" as few partitions (and hence as few peers) as possible, i.e., the partitions should be chosen in a way that minimizes the number of cut graph edges.

6.2 Distributing a structured key space

As already explained, a traffic information system differs in some significant aspects from most of the "classical" peer-to-peer applications such as file sharing systems. In particular, this holds for the very specific request pattern of a traffic information system. Each individual overlay node accesses information about a limited, contiguous part of the road network between the respective car's current position and the destination. This characterizes the subset of the key space a

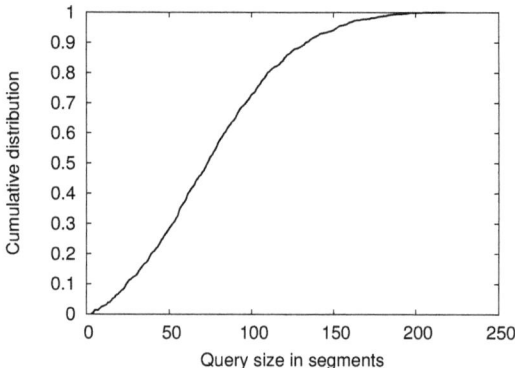

Figure 6.2: Distribution of the query sizes in PeerTIS.

given overlay node is interested in, and thus the interrelation between the queried keys.

We have carried out a simple experiment to illustrate the expected behavior of an application query. Within the same simulation setup as described in Section 5.3.1, we analyzed the queries of the participating cars in the simulation with PeerTIS. Figure 6.2 depicts the cumulative distribution of route lengths queried for. Recall that cars used dynamic navigation and requested information about $a = 3$ alternative routes to the planned destination. From the distribution it can be expected that an average query can comprise more than 100 segments. The cars will be generally interested in multiple, yet contiguous road segments. Thus correlated, non-independent key look-ups for adjacent, consecutive road segments clearly dominate the request traffic. Reducing the effort in answering groups of related requests is therefore vital. In fact, if the aim is an overall reduction of overhead and an overall performance improvement, optimizing non-independent, related follow-up requests is evidently much more important than efficiently handling requests for single, independent keys. We have already seen in the preceding chapter that with a standard DHT, individual look-ups may be efficient—but all keys in a sequence of related look-ups would have to be handled

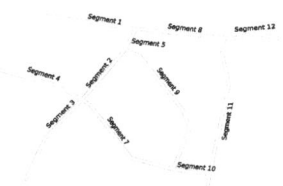 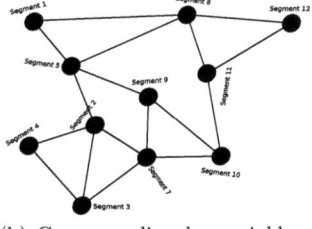

(a) Example road network. (b) Corresponding key neighbor graph.

Figure 6.3: A fragment of a street map and the corresponding key neighbor graph.

separately, and their targets would be spread all over the overlay. Consequently, a considerable number of peers would need to be contacted. In this chapter we follow an alternative design aiming at an overlay structure that allows performing sequences of related queries more efficiently. Basically we pursue the same goal as in the case of PeerTIS but we use more sophisticated methods to achieve it and hopefully avoid the drawbacks.

Here we primarily focus on the question how we should partition the key space between the participating peers, and how these peers should be interconnected. Our aim is simple: we want to be able to answer typical requests of the application with as little effort as possible, and at the same time achieve a reasonable load balancing between the peers.

We will stick to the "classical" design of assigning each key to exactly one peer, as is the basis for the majority of DHTs. Extensions such as redundant assignments to improve aspects like resilience or per-hop latencies [BCM04, RFH+01] have often been discussed and could be integrated in our design, too.

6.2.1 Key neighbor graphs

Two observations constitute the starting point for our considerations. First, we note that the key space in our application is comparatively small. Instead of a large key space (e.g., in a file sharing system the set contains all possible MD5 file hashes and thus 2^{128} distinct keys), the number of keys in our example application equals the number of segments in the road network (about 17 000 in our simulation map). Second, we observe that the key space is very clearly structured; the road network graph provides this structure and characterizes the interdependencies between keys.

We call two keys "neighboring keys" if they are related in the sense that they are likely to be requested together. Consequently, we can describe the relationships between keys by a *key neighbor graph*. The nodes of this graph are the keys. There is an edge between two keys if these keys are neighbors.

Both sets—keys and edges—are known in advance, and we may expect that each peer has them readily available. In the traffic information system application this means that we expect every navigation device to know the street map. Two road segments are neighbors (and are thus connected by an edge in the key neighbor graph) if it is possible to directly drive from one of the road segments to the other one. Note that at a very first glance this is in fact a bit counterintuitive, because the road segments are intuitively considered the *edges* in the road network graph, yet they are the *nodes* in the key neighbor graph. Intersections (the natural *nodes* in the road network), in turn, induce *edges* in the key neighbor graph between all pairs of segments that "meet" at the intersection. This relationship is visualized in Figure 6.3, where Figure 6.3(a) shows a small example road network with a total of 12 segments, and Figure 6.3(b) shows the corresponding key neighbor graph. For instance, segment 8 is connected to segments 1, 5, 11, and 12, so it has edges with these segments in the key neighbor graph.

6.2.2 Partitioning the key neighbor graph

At its core, our overlay design builds directly upon the key neighbor graph. The main concept is to partition the key neighbor graph and to dynamically assign each overlay node to a subgraph. The peers maintain overlay links to the peers which are responsible for neighboring subgraphs, i.e., to those peers that are responsible for a partition that is connected to the peer's subgraph by at least one edge in the key neighbor graph. Queries for connected sets of keys can then "follow" the structure of the key neighbor graph through the overlay. It thus becomes clear that the partitions should be formed in such a way that typical queries "touch" as few partitions (and hence as few peers) as possible.

Therefore, our guideline for partitioning the key neighbor graph between peers should be to keep keys which are often requested together. Consequently, this decision boils down to a graph partitioning problem: dissecting the key neighbor graph into a number of (almost) equally-sized disjoint subgraphs, while cutting as few edges as possible.

In a first attempt, we can indeed stick to this concept and try to minimize the number of edges cut by partitioning the key neighbor graph. Considering our traffic information system application again, we find that it might be worth differentiating further, though: a car on a highway, for example, is typically much more likely to continue traveling on the highway than to take the next highway exit. We can therefore assign edge weights to the edges in the key neighbor graph which reflect how "likely" it is that a queried route actually takes this link. In this case, we aim to partition the graph in a way such that the total weight of cut edges is small.

In our implementation and evaluation, we either use constant edge costs (and thus minimize the number of cut edges) or we assign costs based on traffic densities or road priorities. The latter values are available from the map file used in the simulation. Street segments of OpenStreetMap maps converted to SUMO format posses a set of tags, among them also a field *priority*, describing the "importance" of a road. The values span the range form 2 for small roads in suburbs up to 20 for highways. An excerpt from the map used in the simulation in presented in listing 6.1.

Listing 6.1: Excerpt from the map file.

```
//...//
<edge id="-10426954" from="89155329" to="89155587"
   priority="4" type="highway.residential" function="normal">
<lanes>
    <lane id="-10426954_0" depart="1" maxspeed="13.89"
       length="1.07" shape="2904.43,5557.95 2904.55,5556.89"/>
</lanes>
</edge>
//...//
```

We have also used a more sophisticated method of setting graph weights based on traffic densities: how many vehicles do typically traverse the respective sequence of road segments? The drawback of this approach is that it requires information on the utilization of the road network. Such statistical information on the road network usage could be obtained from the real-world observations that many road authorities perform for the purpose of traffic optimization. For our evaluations, we obtain them by observing the vehicular traffic patterns in a dry run of the simulation.

Given the key neighbor graph $G = (V, E)$ with n vertices V, edges E, and weights $w_{i,j} > 0$ for $(i,j) \in E$, the general graph partitioning problem is to divide the original graph into k (approximately) equally sized subsets $V_1, \ldots, V_k$ such that:

1. $\forall 1 \leq p \leq k : |V_p| \simeq n/k$,

2. $\forall 1 \leq p, q \leq k : p \neq q \Rightarrow V_p \cap V_q = \emptyset$,

3. $\bigcup_{p=1,\ldots,k} V_p = V$,

and the *total edge cut*

$$T := \sum_{(i,j)\in E, i\in V_p, j\in V_q, p\neq q} w_{i,j}$$

is minimal. In our protocol, we will only need the case $k = 2$, i.e., bisectioning into two partitions.

It is known that optimal partitioning is NP-hard [BJ92]. This holds true even if all edge weights are equal, if k is small (even if only a bisection of the graph is sought), and if the maximum vertex degree is limited [BJ92]. However, we can build upon a number of heuristics which have been proposed for finding good graph partitions.

6.2.3 Graph partitioning algorithms

It is not immediately evident which graph partitioning heuristics are well suited to the problem at hand. Existing techniques include spectral methods based on eigenvectors of the graph's Laplacian matrix [HL95], geometric partitioning techniques [GMT95], and graph growing methods [KK98]. The optimal choice will certainly depend on the properties of a specific key neighbor graph. In the following we concentrate on two algorithms: the first one—a combination of graph growing with a refinement algorithm devised by Kernighan and Lin [KL70]—is algorithmically relatively simple, very generic, and nevertheless yields good results. The second one—a geometry-based scheme—is particularly interesting for our example application because it can make use of even more of its specificities. In the following, we outline the basic ideas; for more details we refer the reader to the respective publications.

The combination of graph growing and the Kernighan-Lin algorithm [KK98, KL70] starts in a surprisingly simple and straightforward way: a region around a randomly chosen start vertex is greedily "grown" in a breadth-first fashion, until half of the vertices have been included. Subsequently this initial bisection into subsets A and B is iteratively refined by exchanging vertices between partitions A and B in a specific way. First, so-called D values are calculated for all nodes x:

$$D_x := \sum_{b \in B} w_{b,x} - \sum_{a \in A} w_{a,x},$$

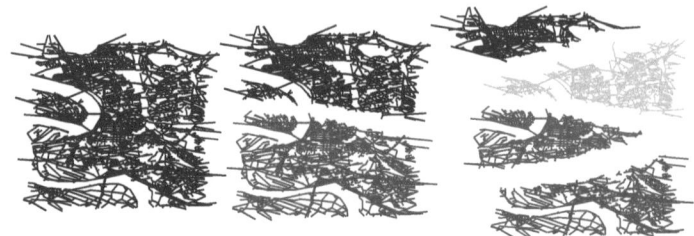

Figure 6.4: Map of Düsseldorf partitioned with KL-GM algorithm.

where $w_{x,y}$ is the edge cost between x and y. Then, out of all pairs (a_1, b_1) where $a_1 \in A$ and $b_1 \in B$, the algorithm identifies the pair where

$$g_1 := D_{a_1} + D_{b_1} - 2w_{a_1,b_1}$$

is maximal. This value corresponds to the largest possible edge cut gain resulting from exchanging vertices a_1 and b_1 between the partitions. In the next step, the pair (a_1, b_1) is put aside and the D values are re-calculated for the remaining nodes in $A \setminus \{a_1\}$ and $B \setminus \{b_1\}$, leading to a second pair (a_2, b_2) with gain:

$$g_2 := D_{a_2} + D_{b_2} - 2w_{a_2,b_2}.$$

The process continues until all nodes are exhausted, resulting in pairs $(a_1, b_1), (a_2, b_2), \ldots, (a_n, b_n)$ and corresponding gains $g_1, g_2, \ldots, g_n$. Quite obviously, the sum of all gains is zero (it is equivalent to exchanging all vertices between the original partitions A and B). Then, the value k is identified which maximizes the partial sum of gains $G_k := g_1 + \ldots + g_k$. The sets $\{a_1, a_2, \ldots, a_k\}$ and $\{b_1, b_2, \ldots, b_k\}$ are exchanged between the partitions. If no k with $G_k > 0$ exists, a (local) optimum has been reached.

Geometric partitioning [GMT95] is interesting for the specific case of our example application because in contrast to other algorithms it can make use of position information, in our case the geographical positions of the road segments. This position information can thereby provide a "hint" on how to partition the graph.[1] The algorithm first projects all $\mathbb{R}^d$ vertices onto the unit sphere centered at the origin in $\mathbb{R}^{d+1}$, along the line connecting the point and the sphere's "north pole" $(0,\ldots,0,1)$. Subsequently, a geometric centerpoint is identified and a specific series of geometric projections is applied. If the resulting set of points is subsequently cut by a random great circle of the $\mathbb{R}^{d+1}$ sphere, this separates the graph vertices into two disjoint, equally sized partitions. While there is no guarantee that the resulting edge cut is minimal, our experience shows that the results are good, especially if the last part of the algorithm is repeated for multiple great circles, keeping the best found solution. It is also possible to improve the edge cut of the obtained partitions by subsequently refining them with the Kernighan-Lin algorithm, as described above. The application of the geometric partitioning refined with Kernighan-Lin on a real map of Düsseldorf is depicted in Figure 6.4.

6.3 Protocol

In the previous section we have introduced the concept of a key neighbor graph and the idea of distributing the keys in a way that naturally supports non-independent queries by following the links in this graph. To this end, we have suggested partitioning the graph and distributing subgraphs to the peers. In this section, we will now fill in more details on how a protocol for our specific example application may look like. In particular, we discuss how look-ups are performed; we also outline how to build and maintain the overlay structure.

6.3.1 Assumptions and overview

As discussed above, the street map can be converted into the corresponding key neighbor graph. By iteratively bisecting this graph with one of the partitioning

---

[1] In a strict sense, this works for overlap graphs; while road networks are not guaranteed to be overlap graphs, they are sufficiently "close" to yield good results.

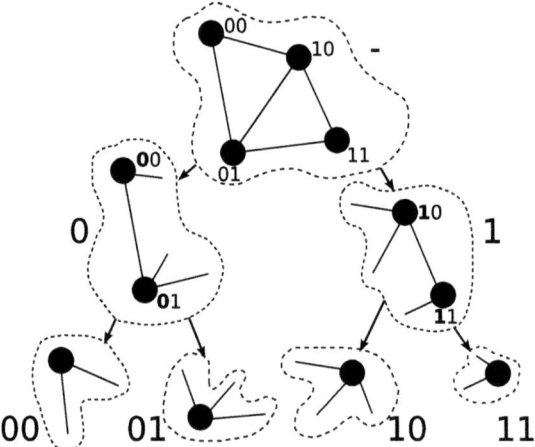

Figure 6.5: Partitioning tree of a graph.

algorithms discussed in the previous section, we obtain a hierarchical structure of subgraphs which we call partitioning tree (see Figure 6.5). The top level of this hierarchy (the root of the tree) encompasses the full graph. It is assigned the empty bit string as a label. This graph is then split into two partitions; the resulting two subgraphs are labeled "1" and "0". Each of those is recursively bi-partitioned further into subgraphs "11", "10", "01", and "00", and so on, until each partition consists of only one node.

This is done only once in advance, before the system is running: the hierarchical partitioning and labeling is constant for a given map, so it may be pre-calculated and stored along with the street map data.[2] The labels of the partitions in the tree uniquely identify one specific partition of the original graph, on a hierarchy level that corresponds to the length of the label. At run-time each peer will maintain all key-value mappings for the subgraph represented by one node in the partitioning tree. Knowing the label of this subgraph is thus sufficient to

---

[2] If the map changes over time, a mechanism would need to be added for sharing map updates re-partitioning the graph accordingly.

fully characterize the set of keys a peer is responsible for.

Furthermore, note that the label for a leaf partition uniquely identifies the one single key that falls into this leaf partition. It can thus be re-used to identify the respective key, as it is already indicated in Figure 6.5. That is, for the traffic information system the leaf partition ID can be used as the globally known road segment ID.

This assignment of IDs has the benefit that it implicitly encodes the hierarchical partitioning of the key neighbor graph so that the partition structure does not need to be stored separately: two road segments are within the same partition after n hierarchical splits if and only if the first n bits of their IDs are equal. Similarly, a key k is part of a partition p of the key neighbor graph (and thus managed by a given peer) if p's label in the partitioning tree is a prefix of k's ID.

Each peer will stay in contact with the peers responsible for neighboring subgraphs of the key neighbor graph to form the overlay. A neighboring subgraph is a partition that is connected to the peer's subgraph by at least one edge in the key neighbor graph. A peer maintaining a neighboring subgraph is called a *neighbor peer*. Thus in our example, the peer responsible for the subgraph "01" will be connected with the peers "00", "10" and "11". It could, however, happen that the subgraph "1" is not yet divided; thus only connection to the peer responsible for the larger part "1" (instead of "10" and "11") would have to be established.

Initially, the overlay structure will consist of only one peer which is responsible for the whole graph. As soon as another peer joins the overlay, the responsibility of the original peer will move down one level in the partitioning tree: it keeps the subgraph labeled "0" and hands over the sibling subgraph "1" to the newly arriving node. Note that there is no hierarchy in the peer structure: once a subgraph has been split, there will be no more peers responsible for the parent node in the partitioning tree.

The overlay structure described here assumes that the key neighbor graph is sufficiently well-connected, and yet can be split into subgraphs without introducing too many links between partitions. This obviously depends on the properties of the key neighbor graph and thus on the specific application. Road networks—the basis for the key neighbor graphs in the application considered here—are "almost" planar graphs (only tunnels or bridges can locally disrupt a road network's planarity). As the promising evaluation results in Section 6.4 will show, this suits the proposed strategy very well.

6.3.2 Locating a single, arbitrary key

Given the overlay structure outlined above, and given an arbitrary key, we now show how the peer can be located that is responsible for maintaining the data associated with this key. Before going into detail, let us summarize what information is available locally to each peer:

1. Each peer maintains one single subgraph of the key neighbor graph (and the corresponding data).

2. It keeps direct network connections to its neighbors, i.e., to those peers whose partitions of the key neighbor graph are connected to its own subgraph by at least one edge.

3. It knows the labels of the subgraphs (and thus the sets of road segments) maintained by its neighbors.

Given this information, a peer that queries a given key first looks at the key neighbor graph—that is, at the street map. It locates the graph node representing the sought-after key. Then, it uses a shortest path algorithm[3] to find the shortest path from that node to any node that is part of any of its neighbors' subgraphs. This identifies the neighbor which minimizes the remaining distance (in terms of the road network) to the destination key. This neighbor is selected as the next hop for the query. The look-up message transmitted to that neighbor includes

---
[3]One might use a generic one like Dijkstra's Algorithm or, in our example application, an algorithm tailored to the specific properties of road networks.

the sought-after key and the address of the node initiating the query. The same process is then repeated by each peer receiving the query, until the destination key is reached. The responsible peer can answer the query directly since contact data of the originator are included in the packet.

This procedure ensures that—out of all the neighbors—always the one which is closest to the target key is selected for forwarding. Evidently, for a connected road network, as long as the responsible peer has not been reached, there must always be at least one neighbor that is closer to the destination.

Intuitively, a query "travels the road network" towards its destination. Note that this indeed suits the partitioning strategy used in the design of the overlay: in Section 6.2.2 we argued that the key neighbor graph is partitioned such that *driving routes through the road network* cross only a few partition borders. This directly translates to *look-up routes along the key neighbor graph* crossing a few partition borders—and thus to a low number of overlay hops.

It would be entirely feasible to calculate the shortest path route only once at the original sender of the query and transmit it along with the query. Recalculating the route at each hop, however, allows to account for local knowledge regarding the overlay topology which is not available at the originator. Despite a high number of simulated peers, we never encountered problems regarding the computational effort for the recalculations.

There is a little twist in the routing of messages when inhomogeneous edge weights are set in key neighbor graph. Shortest paths algorithms try to find the path to the destination with minimal costs, that is the sum of weights of all segments of such a path is minimal among all possible paths between the start and destination. When we set the edge costs according to the priority of the street or density of the cars gained via dry run of the simulation, the routes preferably kept unpartitioned will have high costs. Hence in such cases we set separate edge costs for partitioning and routing: for routing we used the inverse of the partitioning weights.

6.3.3 Requesting a set of correlated keys

Finding the data for a random key is an important function of the overlay; however, as argued before, the efficient processing of queries for sets of consecutive keys is much more important since it clearly dominates the request pattern. The specific strength of our overlay lies in the handling of such queries.

In order to obtain information on a set of consecutive keys, the query originator first needs to locate a peer responsible for one of the keys. This peer—it may be the one responsible for the starting point of a queried route—can be found as described in the preceding subsection.

The list of all searched segments is included in the query that is sent to this first node. Because related segments, which are often requested together, are preferably kept within one partition during partitioning, the first node will often be able to provide information on more than one segment which is then sent back to the originator. The remaining request—with the segment IDs which it cannot answer itself—is forwarded to the respective neighbors. These answer their "share" of the request and then proceed analogously until all the requested information has been completely retrieved. Thus the query, in a sense, follows the queried route through the overlay.

As consecutive road segments correspond to neighbors in the key neighbor graph, they are either handled by the same peer or by peers between which a direct connection exists. Each hop in the overlay will thus allow obtaining information on at least one queried key, and typically more than one. We will investigate this particular fact in our evaluation.

6.3.4 Improving the look-up complexity

The main focus of our work described so far was on the efficient handling of structured queries for correlated segments. The query processing, however, comprised two phases: first the query has to reach the peer responsible for the initial segment of the planned route. Then the query follows the route in the overlay.

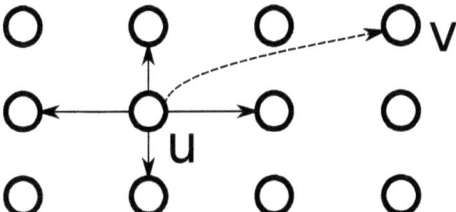

Figure 6.6: Additional edge in a lattice.

While we believe that our design is very good at handling the second part, finding the initial segment is not yet done in an optimal fashion. Assuming that the road network is an (almost) planar graph, we may expect $O(\sqrt{n})$ hops in the overlay before we can enter the second phase, while it is known that other DHTs are able to find a given key in $O(log(n))$ hops (e.g., Chord [SMLN+03], Viceroy [MNR02] or Koorde [KK03]). We now discuss a generic mechanism to improve this initial look-up performance without impeding the second look-up phase.

We looked at the work of Kleinberg [Kle00] as an inspiration. He studied the problem of routing messages on a regular lattice of nodes as depicted in Figure 6.6. His main contribution was a local, greedy routing algorithm with a good expected delivery time. Briefly summarized, he started out by connecting each node to its four direct neighbors in the lattice (depicted as solid arrows). For each node, a single, additional "long range link" to a randomly selected other node v was added (depicted as a dashed arrow). The probability that a given node v is chosen as the target of the additional link is proportional to $[d(u,v)]^{-2}$ where $d(u,v)$ is the distance between u and v measured with Manhattan distance metric. All distances have to be calculated in order to derive the normalization factor N_u of the probability distribution:

$$N_u = \sum_v \frac{1}{d(u,v)^2}$$

The probability distribution function is called inverse r^{th}-power distribution.

The rationale behind this approach is that a message sent in a greedy fashion across the lattice will (with some probability) visit a node with a long-range connection pointing toward the destination of the message. When this happens its path will be shortened significantly. It has been shown that adding a single long-range connection to each node in the lattice yields the expected delivery time of $O(\log^2(n))$ hops. Interestingly, the proposed decentralized algorithm works with a very limited knowledge of the structure of the links in the lattice. In particular, the exact locations of the long-range connections of all nodes do not have to be known. In each step only local information is needed about direct connections and the local long-range link.

In order to apply this idea for GraphTIS we had to solve the problem that in GraphTIS there exists no global view on the structure of the overlay network: peers do not know all the other peers in the network and they do not know how the key space is distributed amongst them. In order to select a target for its long-range link a peer thus needs a way to identify potential targets of additional links, as well as a method to derive the probability distribution used to randomly choose one out of those potential targets. We solve these problems as follows. In each peer, we first determine the center vertex of the part of the key graph managed by it. Then we calculate the distances, i.e., the number of edges that need to be crossed, from that center to all the other vertexes in the key neighbor graph. Assuming a uniform peer distribution of peers in the overlay, this is a good approximation.

This is then used as the distance metric to randomly select one target vertex for a long range link. Probabilities are assigned as in Kleinberg's approach based on the distances to the center vertex. The vertex selected in this fashion will be managed by one peer. This peer can be found by a look-up operation in the overlay and it will become the destination of the long range link. Since joins and leaves of the peers have rendered some long range links obsolete, the process described has to be conducted periodically.

We also looked at an alternative way of improving the overlay structure. This idea was born from the observation that in GraphTIS messages traveling along the graph edges suffer from insufficiencies of the street network: to get from one "end" of the overlay to the other they are limited by the connectivity present in the street network graph. We therefore investigated the idea of "optimizing" the street network graph by randomly adding some "virtual" connections between intersections. These additional connections are added to the street map data known by all the peers. For the purpose of overlay management, graph partitioning, and routing in the overlay, they are used like any "real" connection in the street network. The only difference from real roads is that these virtual connections cannot, of course, be used in driving routes for cars.

Adding such additional random links was inspired by the works of Watts and Strogatz [WS98], who showed that adding just a few random connections in a regular graph can result in so-called "small-world" properties. Our implementation of this idea is quite simple: the original graph was extended by some random edges before the partitioning took place. Everything else with regard to overlay protocol remained as described above.

As already explained, the traffic information system application not only accesses groups of consecutive keys at once but also often accesses the same keys twice or more frequently at different points in time: first during the route planning phase and later again when a road segment is traversed and the observations are uploaded into the distributed data structure. We can use this pattern to improve the performance of repeated look-ups. GraphTIS allows using exactly the same look-up caching as described for PeerTIS in Section 5.2.4.

After the first retrieval of the data for a given key, the address of the responsible peer is known from the response packet. We may thus cache this peer contact information. If the same key or a key close to that key is requested again later on, the respective peer can be contacted directly. In the optimal case, this peer is still on-line and is still responsible for the key so it can answer the request right away. In a less optimal case, the peer is still part of the overlay but is no longer responsible for the key, for instance because in the meantime it has accepted a join request and its subgraph has been split. In this case, though, the contacted peer will typically still be "close" to the queried key in the overlay and may therefore help to find the responsible peer more quickly. In the worst case, the cached peer cannot be contacted any more and the query originator has to fall back to normal query processing (as presented above) after a time-out.

Note that the potentially significant speed-up and network traffic reduction due to successful peer contact caching comes at a very small cost: peers can collect any number of cached IPs as a side effect of their normal look-ups at minimal storage overhead. In contrast to the Kleinberg connections case, there is no need to stay in contact with cached peers as their presence is not necessary for the structural integrity of the overlay. The only possible performance penalty results from waiting for the (adjustable) timeout in the case of a cached peer that can no longer be reached. It is perfectly tolerable for the application if such a delay sometimes occurs before an observation on a road segment is uploaded to the overlay.

6.3.5 Overlay maintenance: join, leave, and recovery

As indicated above, we stay close to known concepts when it comes to maintaining the overlay. In particular, we adapt the respective mechanisms from the CAN overlay [RFH+01] for join, leave, and recovery from node failures. They are well understood and, though originally designed for a hierarchical subdivision of a Cartesian space, they can quite easily be adapted to a hierarchically bi-partitioned key neighbor graph. We only outline the mechanisms here, because the details are equivalent to what has been discussed for PeerTIS.

In order to join the overlay, a new peer obtains the address of at least one active peer by an arbitrary bootstrapping mechanism. It then sends a join request to this peer. The request is forwarded towards a random position in the overlay (that is, to a randomly chosen road segment). The peer currently responsible for that segment splits its subgraph according to the hierarchical bisecting algorithm and hands over one half to the new peer, along with the stored data for the respective keys and with information on the relevant neighbor peers, to which the newly arriving node can then set up overlay connections. To improve the load distribution we employ a mechanism analogous to CAN's volume balancing [RFH+01]. Upon reception of a join request, a peer may check if it knows a peer that is responsible for a larger subgraph. In this case, the query is greedily forwarded to peers with larger and larger subgraphs until it reaches a (local) optimum, where a split finally takes place.

Also Geojoins can be used in GraphTIS as proposed in Section 5.2.3. Instead of joining at a random position in the key space, peers may join the key space of the overlay in an area close to their *own current geographical location*. This results in an improved initial look-up performance because the planned route will start at the current position of the car and the new peer has joined the overlay close to this position. In GraphTIS there is no danger of creating empty zones in the overlay. Potentially each zone can store some data. The main reason to use Geojoins in GraphTIS would be to improve load distribution by reducing "hot spots" but also to speed up the look-up. When using Geojoins areas with high traffic density will be automatically partitioned in smaller subgraphs (reducing the load of individual peers). Directly after joining the network, the new peer will typically fetch all the data needed to make its routing decision. Since the distance between a peer issuing a request and the peer able to answer its first part depends on their distance in the key space, we introduced the concept of geographical joins to minimize this distance and thus accelerate the look-up.

Leaving peers and recoveries from peer failures can be handled directly if there is a "sibling node" that is responsible for the full subgraph with an ID prefix that differs only in the last bit from the leaving peer's responsibility zone label. In that case, the subgraphs can easily be merged, handing over the responsibility to the remaining sibling. If there is no sibling node (that is, if the respective neighbor subgraph has been further partitioned), a leave request is sent towards the smallest known neighbor. Upon reception of such a request, a node checks whether it has a sibling node; if not, the message is forwarded, again to the smallest neighbor. Note that each node must either have a sibling or a neighbor which is responsible for a smaller subgraph. Thus, the request must at some point reach a peer which can merge zones with its sibling; this peer will do so and will then take over the leaving peer's responsibility area. Alternatively to forwarding the request, one of the direct neighbors could temporarily take over the subgraph of the leaving peer and for some time maintain two subgraphs. Upon a join request one of the zones will then be passed to the new peer. Such a simplification will speed up the leaving process and thus reduce the probability that the data maintained by the leaving peer will be lost (for instance because the navigation device is switched off at the end of the journey).

For failure detection, peers exchange periodic hello messages with their neighbors. Each hello incorporates the peer ID and the list of its direct neighbors. If a peer misses a number of periodic hellos from one of its neighbors, a node failure is assumed and a recovery strategy is utilized to restore a consistent overlay structure. To this end, once again just like in PeerTIS, all peers keep track of their two-hop neighbors in the overlay (without actively maintaining overlay connections to them, just by evaluating regular hellos of the direct neighbors). A peer which detects a node failure informs all the neighbors of the failed peer about the problem. If the failed peer had a sibling neighbor it is asked to take over the abandoned area. Otherwise, the detector itself will do so. Of course, a failure of the node would mean that the data from its responsibility subgraph will be lost.

6.3.6 Look-up complexity

Before we come to the empirical, simulation-based assessments, we may ask the question what behavior we should expect from an analytical, asymptotic perspective. Because the overlay is based on the specific key neighbor graph, there is obviously no general answer. Nevertheless, as argued above, road networks are "almost planar", and the peers' partitions will typically be consecutive subgraphs of a similar size. We may thus expect an asymptotic routing complexity that resembles that found in a partitioned two-dimensional plane: routing to a single, random key in $O(\sqrt{n})$ steps, and an asymptotically constant number of neighbors. When using Kleinberg connections we reduce the complexity of the initial look-up to $O(\log^2(n))$ hops.

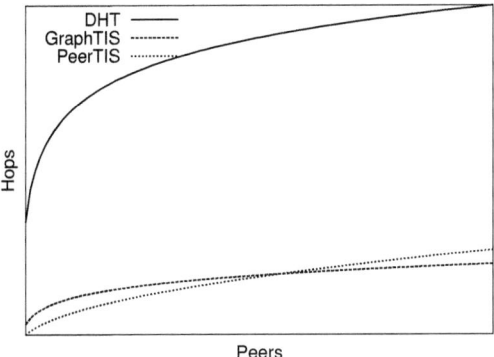

Figure 6.7: Asymptotic number of hops needed to retrieve information on 100 segments length route.

As argued before, however, the more relevant question is for the effort to request information on a group of k consecutive segments. We have already stated that requesting an additional consecutive segment requires at most one additional hop. Querying k segments thus requires a total of $O(\sqrt{n}+k)$ or $O(\log^2(n)+k)$ steps. This stands in sharp contrast to a classical logarithmic-look-up DHT which requires $O(k \log n)$ steps to retrieve information on k keys.

In order to get a feeling for what such a complexity means in reality we plotted the asymptotic number of hops that will be needed to retrieve complete information about a route of $k = 100$ segments with an increasing number of peers in the network. Figure 6.7 shows the results for a classical DHT, PeerTIS and GraphTIS with Kleinberg connections.

6.4 Evaluation

So far we have motivated our work with the statement that distributed (key,value)-storage should be tailored to the application needs when the query pattern is not random and uniform. In particular, we discussed the case of a cooperative distributed peer-to-peer traffic information system and its specific pattern of interrelated queries. In this section, we simulate this application with a realistic vehicular traffic simulator on a real-world street map, and assess the performance of different overlay variants. This includes results from a realization based on Chord [SMLN+03] and CAN [RFH+01]—as representative DHTs—and several variants of the key-graph partitioning overlay as we propose it. We shall also compare GraphTIS with the previously presented PeerTIS.

6.4.1 Simulation setup

We implemented the proposed algorithms and protocols in the peer-to-peer simulator OverSim [BHK07], which we coupled with a road traffic simulator SUMO [KHRW02]. The simulation setup did not change in comparison to the evaluation of the PeerTIS in Section 5.3.1: we have used the same map and the same car traces. The only important modification was to make the partitioned street graph available to all peers. The partitioning was conducted "off-line", that is before the simulation, with separate programs written for this purpose. The results of the particular partitioning were encoded in the graph in form of node labels as described in Section 6.3. Each peer only had to keep track of the number of splits of its zone (its level in the partitioning tree).

For the routing shortest path algorithm, an implementation of Dijkstra's Algorithm from the Boost Graph Library (BGL) [BGL] was used. Also BFS partitioning was implemented with the `breadth_first_search` algorithm from this library.

6.4.2 Comparison with generic DHTs

In the first step of our evaluation we compare the performance of GraphTIS overlays to a realization of the application on the basis of the well-known DHTs: Chord (we used OverSim's implementation of Chord) and CAN.

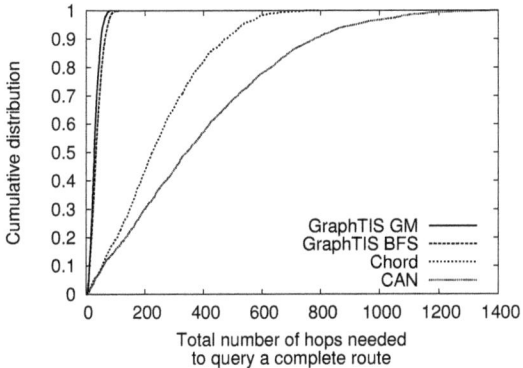

Figure 6.8: Total number of hops needed to query a complete route.

The results of the first comparison are shown in Figure 6.8. The figure shows the cumulative distribution of the total number of hops needed to answer a query for a car's full route, for Chord, CAN and for key-graph partitioning based on various different graph partitioning algorithms, as described in Section 6.2.3. In this part of the evaluation we will only use basic partitioning algorithms: geometric partitioning (GM) and the breadth-first search-based approach (BFS).

The lines for the individual partitioning algorithms for key neighbor graph overlays are so close together that they are hard to distinguish in Figure 6.8. However, all of them evidently achieve far better results than the Chord- or CAN-based variants of the application. The clear dominance of our scheme (regardless of the partitioning algorithm) is not surprising given that Chord needs 4–5 hops on average to locate a single segment in the network. For a car's full route, this results in a quite large total number of overlay hops to retrieve all the information. Clearly, overlays that are optimized for fast look-ups of independent, "random" queries are not the best choice for applications with structured queries.

In DHTs locating one segment of the route does not help in locating further segments of the same route. In our network connected segments can be looked up together, which greatly reduces the overall effort. Furthermore, the preservation

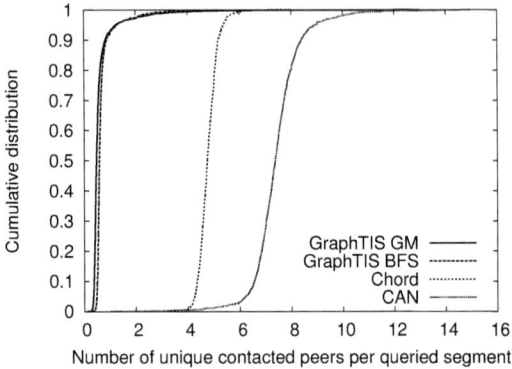

Figure 6.9: Average number of unique peers contacted per queried segment.

of the road networks' structure in our system increases the probability that a single peer is responsible for more than one segment of the query. Thus, one hop in the overlay can well result in the retrieval of more than one data item.

Admittedly, it may be possible to modify Chord further, for instance by aggregating queries that use the same outgoing finger or queries with similar hashes into one message. To assess the potential gains of such an improved query transmission scheme, we show the average number of distinct peers involved in handling a complete query for a full route, divided by the number of road segments on the route (i.e., the number of peers contacted per queried segment). If a peer was involved in processing more than one of the sub-queries (by either forwarding or answering it) it was counted only once. Figure 6.9 shows that even a DHT tweaked in this way is vastly outperformed by our scheme, again regardless of the specific graph partitioning algorithms. Our scheme contacts on average less than 0.4 unique peers for each queried road segment, while Chord needs to query on average more than 2 peers, and CAN more than 8.

These results underline the fact that the distribution of related data all over the overlay in a DHT like Chord or CAN is highly problematic because it results in a high number of peers that need to be contacted in order to retrieve a set

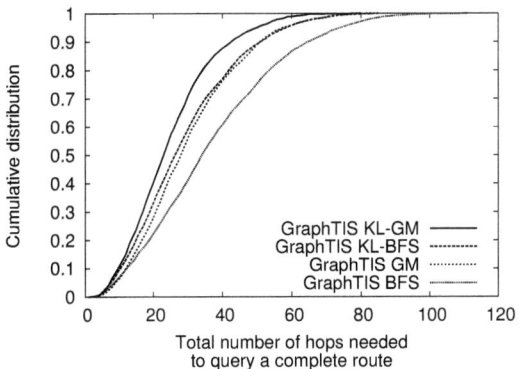

Figure 6.10: Total number of hops needed to query a complete route (zoomed).

of related data items. A large number of hops in the overlay directly translates to longer times a peer has to wait until its query is completely answered. In the case of a traffic information system such a delay is crucial, particularly for the first routing decision. We cannot expect a driver to wait for a longer time before starting his or her journey because the navigation device is waiting for a description of possible routes. Our main design goal was to minimize the delay and thus improve the user experience of a future system.

6.4.3 Choosing the partitioning algorithm

Figures 6.8 and 6.9 have already indicated that the specific key neighbor graph partitioning approach has a little impact on the number of overlay hops for a look-up: in both figures the lines were very close together. This is confirmed at closer examination. Figure 6.10 shows a "zoomed" version of Figure 6.8 (with a reduced x range). We also wanted to assess the influence of the refinement of the partitioning with the Kernighan-Lin algorithm. Thus two new lines are added: "GraphTIS KL-GM", and "GraphTIS KL-BFS". In both cases the application of KL refinement brings significant improvements.

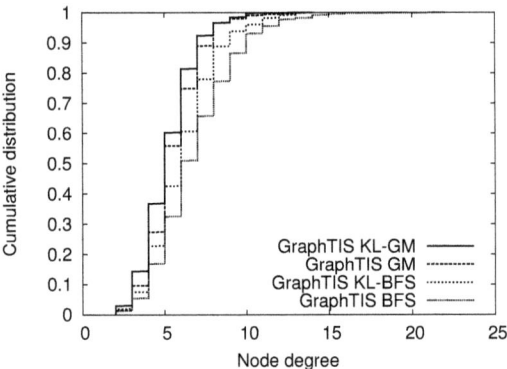

Figure 6.11: Node degree distribution.

The average node degree in the overlay is an important aspect of each overlay design, and thus also of choosing the partitioning algorithm. In our case, in contrast to classical DHTs the degree is not defined *a priori* but results from the partitioning algorithm used. Figure 6.11 shows a cumulative distribution plot of the numbers of neighbors of the peers. The plot is generated from a snapshot of routing tables at the end of the simulation. In our design a higher number of neighbors directly translates into a higher cost for periodic hello messages that need to be exchanged with all direct neighbors and a higher maintenance overhead. On the other hand, small values may reduce the robustness of the system: if only a small number of peers active in the overlay is known, each failure can inhibit proper look-up processing. The distributions presented for all algorithms is acceptable though, as the average number of direct neighbors is not too high so as to cause significant overhead. Only in case of BFS algorithm we observed a single pathological case of producing a partition with relatively high number direct neighbors (over 20 of them).

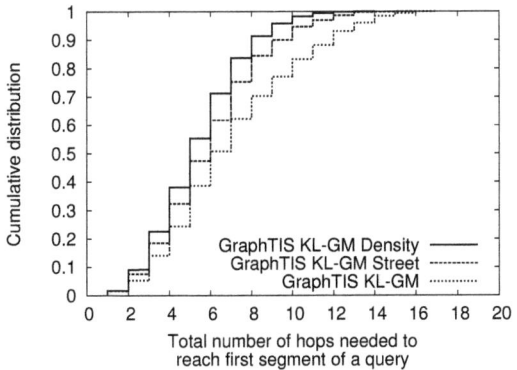

Figure 6.12: Effects of external edge weights (KL-GM).

6.4.4 External edge weights

In our further experiments we have also examined the influence of setting edge weights in the partitioned graph. We used three approaches: constant weights for all edges, weights set accordingly to street priorities obtained from the map file, and weights reflecting traffic densities on the segment. The densities were generated in a dry run of the simulation (without dynamic routing). Of course the edge weights are only relevant for partitioning refined with the Kernighan-Lin algorithm.

When using variable edge weights, we could only see improvements in the performance of the initial look-up processing. That is, with external edges the messages were brought faster to the peer responsible for the first segment of the queried route but the impact on overall performance was limited. The respective results are presented in Figures 6.12 (for KL-GM partitioning) and 6.13 (for KL-BFS). Apparently setting the values led to preserving longer parts of "highways" in the partitioning process. If a query reached a peer responsible for such a long part of a highway it advanced significantly in its progress towards the destination with only one hop.

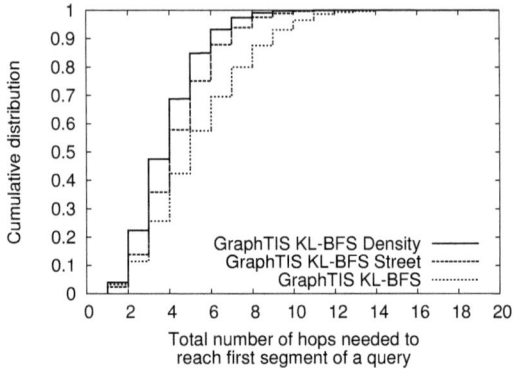

Figure 6.13: Effects of external edge weights (KL-BFS).

In our simulation peers do not prefer streets with higher priorities to drive on (but rather used reported driving speed on segments to optimize their route decisions). Furthermore they naturally avoided streets with high car densities (as they are potentially congested). Thus the second part of query processing was not positively influenced by setting external edge weights: routes interesting to the peers were "preferably" partitioned. Recall here that in our simulations each navigation unit periodically requested descriptions of current and alternative routes. Even assuming that the query regarding the current route was processed more quickly in graphs with inhomogeneous edge weights, the queries for alternative roads nevertheless usually included smaller streets which were preferably cut during the partitioning. Clearly the metric used for setting the edge weights did not reflect all the interests of the cars.

The graph partitioning algorithms that we used in our experiments were not developed with any kind of peer-to-peer networks in mind. These results show us that the specific partitioning algorithms used hardly affect the performance of the system at large; this is also confirmed by all of our remaining results. In particular, it appears to be of surprisingly little value to put much effort into fine-tuning the algorithms by using, e. g., traffic density-based edge weights.

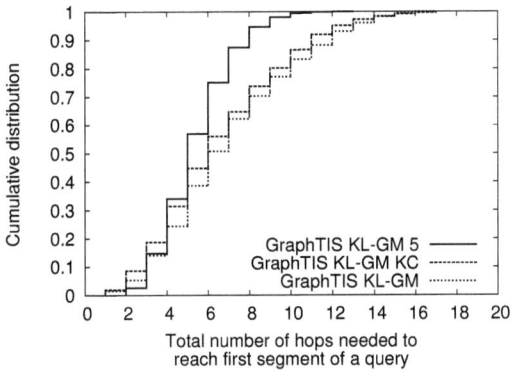

Figure 6.14: Effects of additional connections.

6.4.5 Improvements of the initial look-up

The follow-up phase of processing a query is conducted quite efficiently in our network due to the fact that the structure of the data is preserved. Further improvement of query processing in our design can be achieved by speeding up the look-up of the first segment of the route with the aforementioned improvements.

We first examine the impact of Kleinberg connections and extra random edges on overall performance. The impact of introducing additional edges, as discussed above, is investigated in the plot showing the number of hops needed to reach the initial segments of the requested route. Figure 6.14 shows that Kleinberg connections indeed improve the look-up of the first segment (label "KL-GM KC"). However, additional random edges introduced in the key graph perform even better. Adding as little as five extra connections in the graph can speed up the look-ups significantly. We have actually examined the possibility of adding a larger number of edges in the graph but the gains for higher values were not significant; in addition, additional edges can confuse the partitioning algorithm, leading to substantial changes in the node degree distribution.

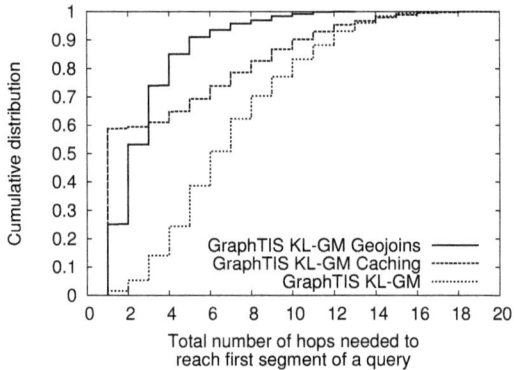

Figure 6.15: Effects of peer contact caching and Geojoins.

Additional edges will work with any type of application built upon a graph-based overlays. We have also proposed a few improvements which are specific to a traffic information application. Application specific improvements of the initial look-up include the caching of previous look-ups (similarly to that proposed for PeerTIS in Section 5.2.4) and Geojoins from Section 5.2.3. In the first case we took advantage of the fact that peers often look up the same road segments multiple times—either in order to stay up-to-date with the changing traffic conditions, or when their own measurements are published for previously queried segments. Directly after joining the network, the new peer will typically fetch all the data needed to make its routing decision. Since the distance between a peer issuing a request and the peer able to answer its first part depends on their distance in the key space we introduced the concept of geographical joins to minimize this distance and thus accelerate the look-up. Instead of joining at a random position in the key space, peers may join the key space of the overlay in an area close to their *own current geographical location*.

Figure 6.15 shows the cumulative distribution of the number of hops needed to localize the first segment of a route. We used KL-GM as a basic variant in order to examine the influence of the proposed adjustments. The examination shows

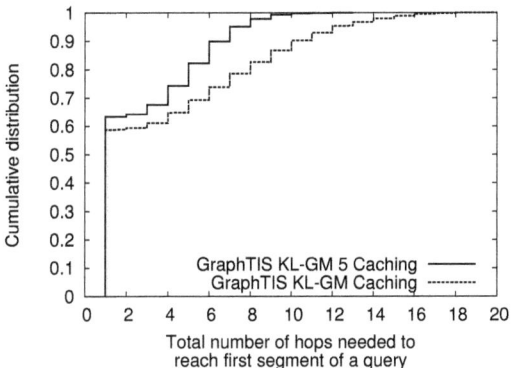

Figure 6.16: Effects of simultaneous peer contact caching and Geojoins.

that, with caching, the first segment of a route can be reached immediately (in one hop) in the vast majority of cases. Geojoins speed up the initial look-up as well.

However, both approaches exhibit some shortcomings. Geojoins yield a more complex join procedure: the join request of the new peer first has to be sent towards the region in the key space containing its current physical position, which may involve many hops and thus induce a delay. As we have already explained, this initial delay will significantly limit the user experience of the final system. Caching works well when the temporal correlations between users' actions can be observed. But particularly in cases of rapid changes in the traffic situation this is not necessarily the case: peers will then search for alternative routes and will have to look up segments which were not previously searched for.

In contrast to Geojoins, caching can be successfully applied simultaneously with extra edges in the graph. Both approaches work well in synergy, as can be seen in Figure 6.16.

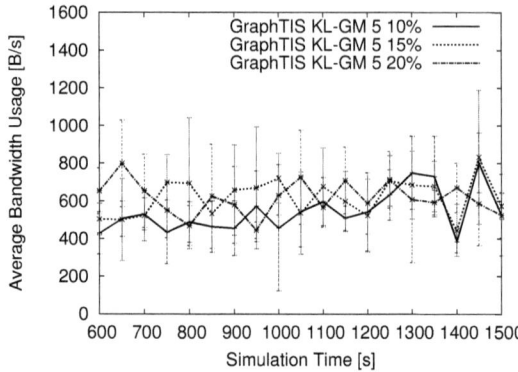

Figure 6.17: Scalability: Average peer bandwidth usage.

6.4.6 Scalability

To assess the scalability of the proposed system, we tested it in simulations with increasing penetration ratios. For each penetration ratio we conducted three simulations. We present the average bandwidth usage over a time span of 1 000 s simulation, after the system has stabilized. At the start of the simulation all the initially present participating cars join the overlay (this artificial effect will not occur in reality). Thereafter, the number of joins and leaves matches the realistic road traffic in the city. Secondly, initially there are very few measurements stored in the network and so the bandwidth usage is naturally smaller. The error bars show 95 % confidence intervals. As can be seen in Figure 6.17, the impact of varying penetration ratios on the average bandwidth usage per peer is negligible.

6.4.7 Comparison with PeerTIS

The last part of our evaluation is a direct comparison between PeerTIS and GraphTIS. For the sake of clarity, in the remainder of this section we will focus

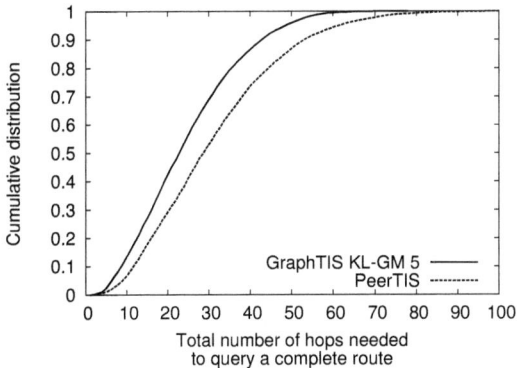

Figure 6.18: Total number of hops needed to query a complete route: differences between PeerTIS and GraphTIS.

on the results from one specific partitioning algorithm, i.e., KL-GM 5.

A comparison of the performance of PeerTIS and GraphTIS in terms of hop count is depicted in Figure 6.18. The overall difference is not considerable but a slight advantage of GraphTIS can be observed. Basically both systems pursue the same goal: they try to preserve the known structure of the data. However, they use different means to achieve the goal, and apparently both approaches work quite well as far as look-up processing is concerned.

We now examine the induced network load, both for data traffic and for overlay maintenance. Figure 6.19 shows the average bandwidth usage in the whole network. The error bars show 95 % confidence intervals. For each simulation second we added up the sizes of all messages exchanged in the network. As application data we classified queries and look-ups (generated or forwarded by the peers), responses, and traffic caused by handing over data upon joins or leaves. The maintenance overhead comprises all application-data independent traffic, like periodic hellos or join and leave requests.

The bandwidth consumption in both cases is quite small, and easily achievable with mobile Internet access networks like UMTS or GPRS. GraphTIS uses more

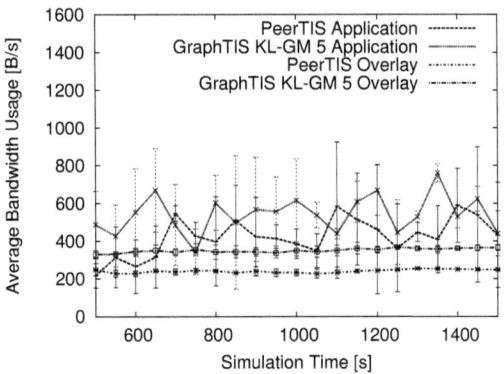

Figure 6.19: Average bandwidth usage in the network.

bandwidth for overlay maintenance. However, the maintenance overhead is quite stable over time and at an acceptably low level. This can be traced back to the quite reasonable distribution of routing table sizes in the network (Figure 6.11). There is no significant difference between the amounts of traffic caused by application data.

We have also observed that the bandwidth usage of GraphTIS depends on the algorithm used for partitioning. It was noticeably smaller for geometric partitioning without Kernighan-Lin and without extra edges (not presented in the plot for reasons of clarity), but then it did not perform so well in terms of look-up efficiency. The maintenance overhead is proportional to the number of direct neighbors. This is the usual trade-off in peer-to-peer systems: a smaller routing table means less maintenance overhead but results in less efficient routing of look-up messages.

The second metric used for workload estimation is the amount of data stored on the peers. The cumulative distribution of the data collected after 30 minutes of a simulation is depicted in Figure 6.20 (we considered measurements that are older than 30 minutes as too old to be of significant value for a traffic information system, and so older measurements are removed). The unfair load balance was

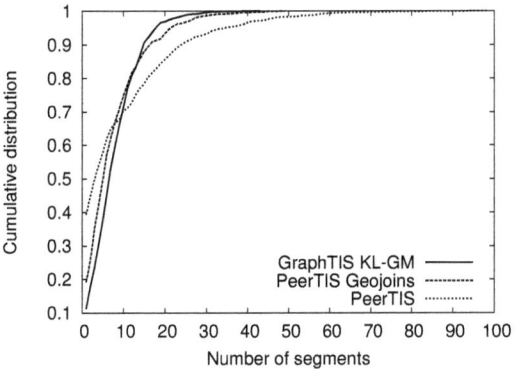

Figure 6.20: Load distribution in the network.

the main motivation to develop the graph-based overlay. As we can see GraphTIS exhibits a very good load-distribution which is much better than the original PeerTIS. It even outperforms the modified PeerTIS with Geojoins. Actually, the load distribution of GraphTIS is on a par with generic DHTs despite the fact that the latter uses consistent hashing for uniform data placement while GraphTIS does not.

6.5 Conclusion

In this chapter we presented a new peer-to-peer overlay structure tailored for special needs of traffic information systems. It specific supports a key space where the interrelation of the keys can be described by a graph (street graph in our case). We demonstrated that this resulted in excellent look-up performance. Furthermore, the use of a graph instead of a map (as in PeerTIS) to distribute the data allows to avoid unfair load distribution. In fact, we achieved a load distribution comparable with that of a hash-based system.

Chapter 7

Application Evaluation

Traffic information systems (TIS) provide navigation units with information about the current traffic conditions and thus enable dynamic routing decisions. We started our research in this area at the network layer and showed that VANETs are not the best solution for such a system. Then we proceeded upwards in the ISO OSI layer model and investigated a possible peer-to-peer basis for TIS applications. We have presented two different approaches: one based on an adjusted DHT (PeerTIS) and an overlay using a graph-based data placement scheme (GraphTIS). In this chapter we conclude our work by examining the application layer in a more detailed fashion.

The focus of existing work has mainly been on the technical feasibility of the solutions proposed so far, e.g., dealing with the constrained bandwidth and limited connectivity of communication networks. The feasibility of a technical solution is certainly an important factor. But, as far as market introduction is concerned, it is even more important to show that such a system, when in place, can really bring some added value to the users. In our case this would primarily be the possible improvements in travel times.

Given this background, our contributions are twofold. We extend the previously proposed peer-to-peer structure by adding a publish/subscribe mechanism to handle updates efficiently and show how dynamic routes can be calculated efficiently in this setting. Finally, and potentially most importantly, we assess the benefits—i.e., travel time reduction—that a user will obtain from using our system.

7.1 Related work

7.1.1 User benefits in cooperative traffic information systems

We have already presented a wide spectrum of solutions for collecting and exchanging information about traffic conditions. Ideas for the technical realization of such systems range from fully distributed approaches based on local, immediate wireless communication via vehicular ad-hoc networks (VANETs), to infrastructure-based centralized solutions. We will first look at the works on traffic information systems and review their contribution with regard to assessing the potential user wins such systems can offer (regardless of their technical realization details).

Works using historical floating car data [PBB+08, YLSW10] cannot assess the real potential of traffic information systems. The authors have used FCD collected by taxis and treated them as if they were available in a traffic information system. A comparison of the real taxi driver routes with the optimal routes determined with regard to traffic conditions has show that significant improvements in travel time are possible when using a TIS. But there is no guarantee that the estimated optimal times are really achievable in reality. The main limitation of this work is the fact that the evaluation was done "off-line", i.e., cars did not really change their routes and take "optimal" alternatives. Thus the interplay between all the participants, which is precisely what we would like to focus on, was not included in the study.

SOTIS [WER+03] used simulations to evaluate the idea of a VANET-based traffic information system. Their simulation scenario consists of a 160 km long part of a highway with two lanes in each direction. The authors examined the propagation delay of the exchanged data. In such a limited scenario they were unable to prove that the system can bring benefits to the users: there were no alternative routes (and thus no dynamic routing).

CASCADE [IW08a] is another system using a highway scenario without dynamic routing and alternative routes. The speed of information dissemination was examined with a four-lane highway of length 100 km with vehicles enter the highway according to a Poisson distribution and travel at a maximum speed of 30 m/s.

In [XB06] a map of Southern California's Inland Empire freeway network was used. The network included the four major freeways consisting of approximately 500 roadway segments. The authors did not use a separate traffic simulator but rather estimated the accuracy of the information available. The problem of efficient dynamic routing when using such data was not discussed.

Our previous work on PeerTIS [RSKM09] also included an estimation of possible user wins. However, we performed this evaluation off-line. During the simulation a snapshot of the local storages of all peers in the scenario was generated. The data were then used to calculate optimal routes for a selected group of cars. The travel times of the routes were estimated based on the values from the snapshot and subsequently compared with the travel times of the original routes. Such an approach has obvious limitations as it is unable to capture the whole interplay between the system users.

More comprehensive evaluations of a traffic information system use separate traffic simulators to generate a detailed movement of cars in the simulator. An example of such an approach is [GIO04]. The scenario was composed mostly of the highways in southern New Jersey. The network consisted of approximately 4 000 road segments. Car movement was generated with the help of a micro-traffic simulator Paramics [CWM94]. The effectiveness of the proposed solution was tested by simulating an incident on the default route of the simulation. The authors then evaluated how much time was needed for the information about the accident to reach all the participants. A readjustment of the routes was, however, not performed.

Also TrafficView [NDLI04b] was evaluated with the help of a self-implemented traffic simulator `setdes`. The work focused on the average delay of information spread. The scenario comprised a 15 km highway with two lanes in each direction. In contrast to SOTIS, the authors included exits and entries on the highway. Yet, again there was no technical possibility for cars to really use alternative routes as all cars had to stay on the simulated highway.

The works of [LSW+08] included an analysis of travel time savings possible with a traffic information system. The authors used VISSIM [PTV] to simulate vehicular traffic in the city of Brunswick, Germany. The model covers an area of approximately $16\,km^2$, 500 km of roads and a total of about 10 000 cars. VISSIM, however, does not allow to influence the car behavior during the simulation. Thus a simplification of off-line evaluation of the travel times had to be applied. The authors estimate that average travel time improvements of 10 % are possible, and likewise, even for small penetration ratios (that is less accurate information about traffic conditions) gains are still possible.

A realization of a TIS based on mobile Internet communication and centralized servers [SSC+10] also included an estimation of potential user benefits. The authors used SUMO as a traffic simulator and simulated vehicle movement in the area of a large motorway interchange next to Frankfurt Airport. This region of 10 km × 10 km includes two major German motorways (A3 and A5) and one large trunk road (B43). The authors, however, only examined the influence of the proposed traffic information system on the CO_2 emission. The changes in travel times were not reported.

The studies reviewed so far mostly did not include an assessment of potential user gains because the simulation environments were designed to a provide detailed view of the network layer, and the application layer was simplified. A typical abstraction employed was, for instance, a pre-defined car movement which did not change during the simulation — that is, cars did not really react to the available information. There are many limitations of such an approach. On the one hand the travel time estimations are not accurate because some factors influencing the times are not included. For instance, the traffic lights in a city scenario can cause an additional delay.

On the other hand, when no dynamic routing is used, it is questionable if the technical feasibility of a solution is really proved. For instance, dynamic routing could change the densities of cars on a given route (some cars will take an alternative route). This fact can again influence the speed of information dissemination in VANETs. Also the problem of load distribution in peer-to-peer based TIS is partly a side-effect of traffic congestion: streets are overloaded with cars and thus responsible peers are overloaded with data. A traffic information system with dynamic routing can by mitigating one problem (congestion) can also mitigate the other (load distribution). In our evaluation we shall address this as yet unexplored aspect: the coexistence and interplay of application and network.

The main purpose of a cooperative traffic information system is to influence the behavior of the participants by enabling dynamic routing. We believe that a plausible feasibility study should include dynamic routing components, otherwise a number of important factors are not captured.

7.1.2 Decision making

Provided some information about current traffic conditions is available, the drivers have to take routing decisions. This is a complex subject often discussed in the literature.

Ben-Akiva et al. [BAPI91] list possible problems which may appear when taking a routing decision provided with information about traffic conditions:

a) oversaturation (users may feel "overwhelmed" with the data),

b) overreaction (too many drivers respond too quickly to a given information and change their routes causing "oscillations" of a jam between parallel routes),

c) concentration (without a TIS people use different routes determined mainly by the start and destination, whereas with a TIS they are drawn to streets with less traffic, which leads to congestion).

The first problem is a man-machine interaction problem and we will not address it in our work. The reason for overreaction is the rational behavior of the participants: they try to minimize their own travel times. If all drivers behave in the same way they choose the same routes. In order to reduce the risk of an overreaction, [WBKS02] suggested using not only the current travel time on a given segment but also a gradient of the most recently collected values as a metric. Such a gradient can be obtained from our peer-to-peer traffic information system.

The process of a routing decision with available dynamic information on traffic conditions has been described by Wahle et al. [WBKS02]. The authors use simulations with a multi-agent approach. Each agent made decisions on two layers: on the tactical layer (where microscopic movement of a car was used, following the Nagel-Schreckenberg model [NS92]), and on the strategic layer (dynamic agents use the information available to choose one of the alternative routes). The simulation scenario comprised of two routes of equal length. The authors observed that the cars were unable to find the global optimum in travel times, and form a jam on one route or oscillating jams between the routes were observed. The authors suggested that a system where drivers cannot coordinate their decisions will inherently suffer from such shortcomings. However, the exact impact of this fact is not known. Especially in the city scenarios with the number of the alternative routes is higher than two as assumed in this work.

It is important to underline following contradiction: by improving the traffic flow in a street network a TIS might increase some individual travel times. On average the drivers (not only aware of the traffic conditions) are better off. Minimizing individual travel times will increase the density on alternative routes and reduce the flow speed there. Thus cars traveling originally on these alternative routes will reach their destinations later.

Further theoretical works concentrate on different types of the Vehicle Routing Problem (VRP) [YC05, DDS92, FGS04]. They formally describe algorithms for routing cars (understood as managing a fleet of cars) to visit a list of predefined places, e.g., customers, within given time windows when dynamic information about the current traffic conditions [DDS92] or the traffic lights status [YC05] is available. Formal methods use "dynamic" graphs where the graph edges of the network are available only in some time windows (for instance when the traffic light is green) and are removed in other periods (red light). All routes start and end at a given central place. This constitutes a different problem statement than ours, thus we will use a standard shortest path algorithms for determining the routes of individual participants.

7.2 Publish/Subscribe

With the systems proposed so far (PeerTIS and GraphTIS), a car can get information on the current traffic situation along a possible route in an efficient way. What is not easily possible, however, is keeping track of changes of the underlying data. To check whether the currently chosen route is still the best option, a car would have to query the peer-to-peer system periodically. This approach will waste resources whenever traffic conditions have not changed significantly since the last time the information was requested. Thus, in this chapter we would like to examine the applicability of the publish/subscribe paradigm to distribute the updates on traffic conditions. With such an approach it is possible to forgo the communication until something important or meaningful happens instead of undertaking the effort of informing the users that there is no traffic congestion on their routes.

It can be expected that the application of the publish/subscribe paradigm will reduce the bandwidth usage of the discussed application. An important question is, however, if the savings do not come at the cost of less optimal routing decisions. Therefore we discuss and evaluate our publish/subscribe solution together with the dynamic routing, as the both subjects are clearly closely related to each other.

In a publish/subscribe-based system, instead of repeating the request the participants subscribe once for the selected keys. They are then actively informed by the overlay if relevant changes occur. For a general discussion of using publish/subscribe in peer-to-peer networks, we refer the reader to [EFGK03].

Using the taxonomy from [EFGK03], we use a peer-to-peer content-based publish-subscribe system with a hierarchical multicast topology. Peers implicitly subscribe for road segments when they request data about them while performing route planning. Subscription requests are thus regular query packets and they are directly answered with the requested data. In addition to this immediate response, though, the responsible peers also keep track of a list of all the peers that subscribed for the segment. Thus, each peer is a so-called broker for the data concerning the road segments it manages.

The broker of a road segment monitors the incoming data and determines if the traffic conditions on that segment have changed significantly. This is the case when the travel time needed to traverse the road segment changes by more than a given factor compared to the value reported previously (in our evaluation we used a deviation of more than 10%). Such an approach of reducing the communication burden by transmitting only measurements that differ significantly from a "typical" situation has also been used by others [GIO04, DJ07].

To reduce the burden of informing all subscribers, the broker divides the group of peers which will be informed into several equally sized subgroups. Only one representative out of each such group is directly informed. In addition to the actual notification, the messages also contain the addresses of further peers which will be informed. Each representative will then forward the notification to those peers.

We employed a soft-state approach for subscription management: subscriptions have a limited time-to-live after which they are removed from the system. Hence the subscriber has to periodically "refresh" its interests. Another way of removing the subscriptions was triggered by incoming updates: if the originator of an incoming measurement previously subscribed for information about the segment, its subscription was removed. It was assumed that the car just passed the segment and further notifications about the changes are not relevant for the driver. When a broker leaves the network it hands over the list of subscriptions, similar to the way it hands over the traffic data it was responsible for.

7.3 Dynamic vehicle routing

The process of dynamic (re-)routing of vehicles encompasses two phases. First, an initial route to the planned destination has to be found. Second, while the vehicle follows this route, updates on the traffic condition may cause it to change its route.

7.3.1 Initial routing decision

As far as classical navigation is concerned, shortest path algorithms like Dijkstra's shortest path algorithm are used. Unfortunately, though, these algorithms require information on all edge weights. While a peer-to-peer traffic information system can provide the navigation unit with data on any road segment it asks (or subscribes) for, the retrieval of all available measurements each time a routing decision has to be made is not feasible. Thus a challenge is to select and subsequently request only the data important for the routing decision. For that purpose we developed two strategies.

In the first one, the navigation unit determines the static shortest path to the planned destination (not considering the current traffic conditions). Thereafter the information about the current traffic condition on this route is requested and the local weights for that route are updated accordingly. The static values in the map are based on the maximum allowed speed, so these travel times are lower bounds for the real-time values. The returned information can thus only increase the estimated travel time along the calculated route. Hence, the routing is started again after the information has been received, now with static travel times for those route segments not yet queried (those that have not been on the static shortest path), and with real-time travel times for those route segments that have been on the calculated route. If a new shortest path is found, the respective missing data are requested. The process is repeated until the shortest path contains only segments for which dynamic information is available. We call this the *greedy* approach. Because the static travel times are lower bounds, this algorithm is guaranteed to find the route with the currently lowest travel time based on real-time data, but it may happen that a large amount of data needs to be requested in many iterations until the algorithm terminates. In practice, it is therefore advisable to limit the number r of iterations.

An alternative strategy defers the communication until the set of segments that should be queried is fully known. First a set of the static a fastest routes is determined by means of a modified Dijkstra's Algorithm [CMM95]. For these routes the dynamic data are requested. As soon as the data are available, the fastest route out of that subset is selected. We call this approach *AltRoute*.

7.3.2 Keeping in touch with the development of the situation

Since traffic conditions change over time, the drivers have to update their local information to check if the original route decision is still optimal. This is done by either periodically requesting the data for possible routes (in our simulations, cars did so every three minutes) or by subscribing for the data and waiting for notifications, as described in the previous section. As soon as new data become available, the route has to be adjusted. This is done in a similar manner as the first routing decision described above. In order to avoid an overreaction and oscillations, we do the following: if a better alternative route is found when the car is already driving, it will not necessarily change its route. Only when the expected travel time of the alternative route is significantly shorter than the current one, the route is adjusted. By doing so we mitigate to some extent the problem of overreaction.

7.4 Evaluation

7.4.1 Simulation setup

For our evaluation we have used a similar set of tools as in the previous evaluations (see Section 5.3.1 and Section 5.3.1). The set included the peer-to-peer simulator OverSim [BHK07] which we coupled with the road traffic simulator SUMO [KHRW02]. We have used the same map and the same car traces. For the following evaluation it was crucial that SUMO offers a convenient way of interacting with the simulation through its TraCI interface [WPR+08]: not only is it possible to obtain information about the current position of a given car, its planned route, etc. but also to *change* the routes of individual cars. For this evaluation we had to extend this interface by implementing some new functions. In particular we needed to integrate in SUMO the extended Dijkstra's Algorithm, as described in Section 7.3. SUMO natively separates the routing decisions for different cars, that is setting the travel times for a street segment according to the available information influences only the routing decision made by the setting car. The results of the routing can now be fetched via TraCI. The simulation time was 2 400 seconds of road traffic for each simulation run.

For the data exchange we use the same implementations of the peer-to-peer algorithms as in the previous chapters. Specifically, GraphTIS is used with the KL-GM partitioning algorithm and 5 additional edges. The implementation of GraphTIS only has to be extended with a publish/subscribe module. Apart from a storage of traffic measurements each peer also had a storage for maintaining subscriptions. Upon join or leave of peers measurements and subscriptions were handed over. The subscription lifetime was set to 600 seconds.

With regard to user updates we implemented a small improvement. Recall here that previously as soon as a car traversed a road segment, it contributed a measurements of its travel time along that segment. Such a strategy is often utilized in traffic information systems but may lead to the following problem: a traffic jam is only reported after the relevant road section has been completely traversed. This could potentially take a long time, depending on the road condition and the length of the road segment. In extreme cases a traffic jam will be reported after it is completely traversed. We have therefore also use triggered updates: each car estimates the travel time of the segment it is entering and if the traversal takes much more time than expected, a triggered update is sent. The estimation of the travel time is done based on the available traffic measurements or (when no data were available) the segment length and maximal driving speed are used from the street map. We assume that the deterioration of the traffic conditions (that is traffic jams) have a potentially larger impact on the traveling times and thus should be reported as soon as possible.

In order to stay in touch with the current traffic situation along the remaining part of their routes, the peers perform periodic queries once every 180 seconds if periodic requests are used. For publish/subscribe the difference between the reported and the current traffic condition have to change by at least 10 % to trigger a notification to the subscribers. Therefore each time an update is received, the responsible peer has to check if it needs to inform any of the peers that subscribed for that particular segment.

7.4.2 Dynamic routing

We estimated the potential benefits offered by a traffic information system when using different routing strategies: greedy and alternative routes as described in Section 7.3 with travel times generated by a shortest path algorithm without information about the current traffic conditions. The information about car travel times without dynamic routing was obtained from a dry-run of the SUMO simulation. We conducted a number of simulations for a range of reasonable values for parameters r (Greedy) and a (AltRoute). Figure 7.1 shows that the greedy algorithms yields the best results for $r = 4$ rounds. Presumably for higher values the initial routing decision simply takes too much time. Recall that the routing decision is made after all the data are fetched, thus it may happen that in the meantime the car has already got stuck in traffic jams on its original route.

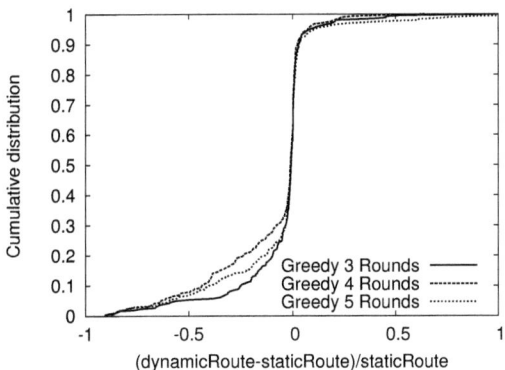

Figure 7.1: Travel times improvement (Greedy).

For the alternative route algorithm (see Figure 7.2), the description of all possible routes is retrieved in simultaneous requests. Thus the process does not necessarily take longer for higher values of a. However, we noticed that the alternatives generated based on the static edge values were very similar to each other. Such alternatives shared many common segments, thus higher values of a increased the basis for a routing decision only by a small fraction. We believe that $a = 3$ offers a good compromise between accuracy of information and bandwidth usage.

A direct comparison between the best performing algorithms is presented in Figure 7.3: the greedy approach with $r = 4$ produced a slightly better distribution of travel times than AltRoute with $a = 3$. Clearly, in both approaches the majority of drivers reach their destinations sooner than with the original routes. There is also a large group of cars which are not influenced by the dynamic routing at all. Admittedly there are also few cars arriving at their destination latter when dynamic routing is used. These are mainly cars with good initial routes which are "disturbed" by the cars using dynamic navigation. The fraction of affected cars is small however, suggesting that the previously mentioned problem of concentration does not play a big role in the city scenarios with multiple alternative routes.

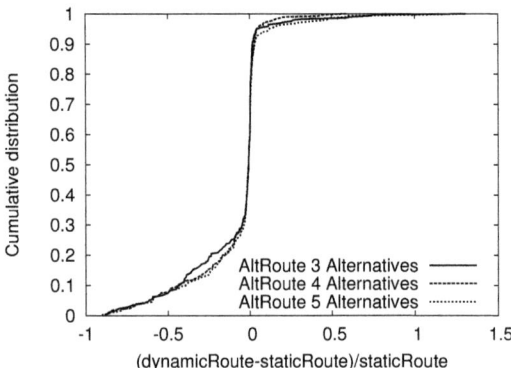

Figure 7.2: Travel times improvement (AltRoute).

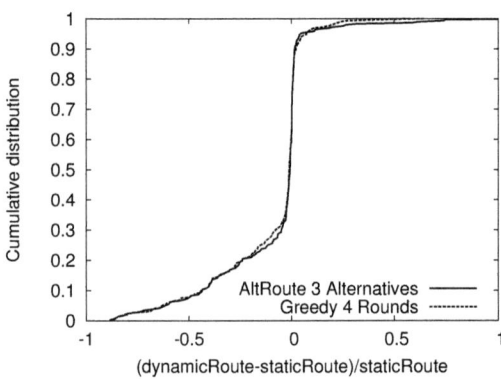

Figure 7.3: Comparison of travel times improvement.

We may now say that the possible gains our system can offer are known; what are then the costs? A possible metric for that is the bandwidth usage of the best performing algorithms (that is AltRoute with $a = 3$ and Greedy with $r = 4$). The greedy algorithm causes a slightly higher bandwidth usage in the network. To illustrate this we summarized the size of all packets sent in each simulation second. The mean load over time plot is presented in Figure 7.4, including 95 % confidence intervals from three independent simulation runs. We have also conducted experiments showing that the bandwidth usage of the greedy algorithm is higher than that of AltRoute even if $a = r$. The reason why the greedy algorithm requests more data than the alternative routes approach is as follows: Since the measured travel times provided by the cars are, in most of the cases, worse than the static values, each communication round generates a different route (comprised mainly of segments for which no data are available). The routes produced by the alternative routes algorithm, on the other hand, were often very similar to each other and before sending a query we removed segments contained in other queries sent in the same round.

The values presented in Figure 7.4 are slightly higher, compared to the results of bandwidth usage of GraphTIS presented in the previous chapter. The slight increase is caused by triggered updates.

We were also able to observe a rather interesting interrelation between the changes in road traffic caused by the TIS and the structure of the overlay. For example, due to the dynamic routing decisions many formerly unused road segments are traversed. This increases quite substantially the number of keys managed by the peer-to-peer system. At the same time the average storage size remains unchanged, i.e., the measurements are spread over a larger number of road segments. In consequence we are convinced that any simulation environment which does not include the feedback loop between application and network (i.e., rerouting of vehicles based on the information gathered from the TIS) is unlikely to capture the full complexity of this environment.

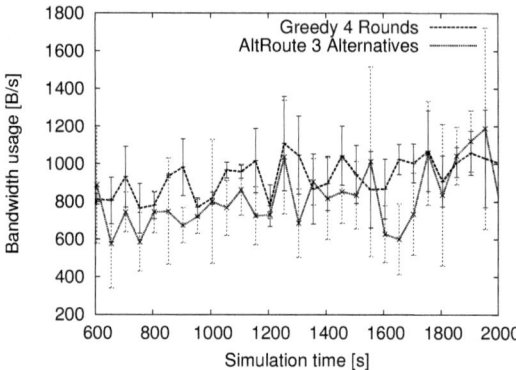

Figure 7.4: Total bandwidth usage caused by the application.

7.4.3 Publish/Subscribe

The integration of a publish/subscribe module in GraphTIS aimed primary at reducing the bandwidth usage caused by the traffic information system application. The difference in bandwidth usage between systems relying on periodic queries and publish/subscribe is depicted in Figure 7.7 and Figure 7.8, for greedy ($r = 4$) and alternative routes (with $a = 3$) respectively. Especially in the former case a substantial reduction of the induced network load can be observed. As already explained, the greedy algorithm requests a lot of data in each routing round, constantly searching for better routes. When using publish/subscribe the main effort is put in the initial route decision, afterward only notifications (and subscription refresh) cause network usage.

The savings in bandwidth, however, come with less optimal routes. This is due to the fact that the traffic conditions on a segment have to change significantly before this change is reported to the subscribers. For our choice of the threshold (10 %) the impact can be seen separately for the Greedy and AltRoute algorithms in Figure 7.5 and Figure 7.6. It should be noted that this is a trade-off: for both

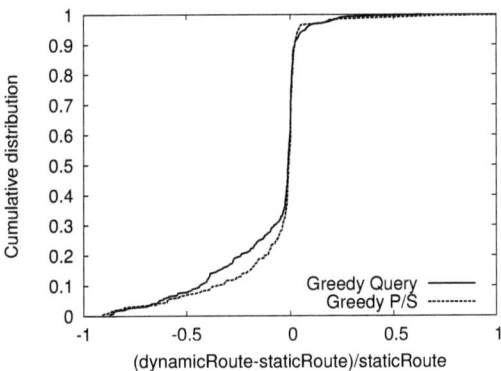

Figure 7.5: Publish/Subscribe: Travel time improvements (Greedy).

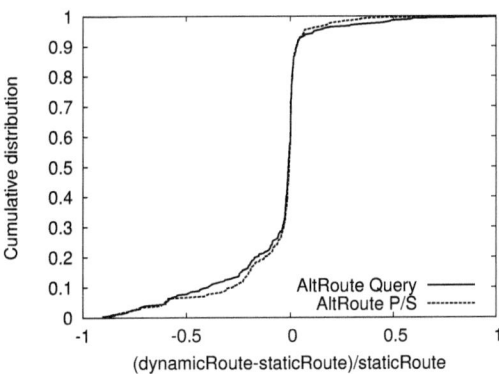

Figure 7.6: Publish/Subscribe: Travel time improvements (AltRoute).

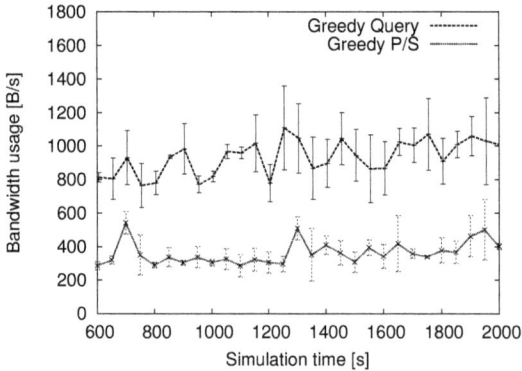

Figure 7.7: Publish/Subscribe: Bandwidth usage (Greedy).

periodic requests and publish/subscribe bandwidth can be saved by accepting less accurate road traffic information.

Broadly speaking, when publish/subscribe is used, cars mainly react to deterioration on their current route, being notified each time such an event occurs, whereas the query-based system tries to periodically improve the route.

7.5 Conclusion

In this chapter we have modified our architecture of the peer-to-peer based traffic information system by adding a component to efficiently handle updates regarding the traffic situation. In our approach we took into account the special properties of traffic information systems. Furthermore, by employing dynamic routing of vehicles we were able to investigate the benefit that a user can expect from using this system and to identify interesting effects such as the interplay between the structure of the overlay and the real-world traffic conditions influenced by the application using the overlay.

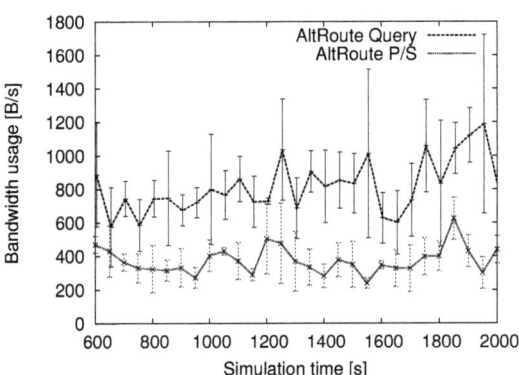

Figure 7.8: Publish/Subscribe: Bandwidth usage (AltRoute).

Chapter 8

Conclusions

In this thesis we have discussed the subject of inter-vehicular communication with an emphasis on traffic information systems. We have proposed a scalable solution to share and distribute traffic related data among cars. By doing so we have also identified and solved a number of interesting problems with special regard to this particular application.

We started our work in Chapter 2 with a review of related works on traffic information systems. This review allowed us to formulate a technical specification of the discussed system together with its unique communication characteristics. In a cooperative TIS the participating cars are not only consumers of information but they also produce information by sharing their observations (such as local measurements of the current traffic conditions) with other vehicles. Such a cooperative approach allows for collecting a large amounts of data at a relatively small cost. Instead of deploying an expensive, dedicated measuring infrastructure, information that is already available on board is shared (such as the current position and driving speed). The application possesses a very characteristic communication pattern. A TIS usually requires communication among many participants spread over relatively large distances that can span from ten kilometers in the case of a city scenario up to a hundred kilometers on highways. Hence the communication requirements of the TIS applications are quite challenging: continuously updated data measured by a large number of system participants is to be made available to many vehicles in a relatively large area.

Equipped with the defined communication requirements of the discussed application we show in Chapter 3 that the current approach of implementing a TIS in Vehicular Ad-Hoc Networks (VANETs) inherently suffers from the bad connectivity and limited capacity of wireless ad-hoc networks. In particular, we have developed a formal framework to evaluate the proposed VANET solutions and assess the amount of data reduction needed to make them scalable. We have shown that some of the proposed solutions do not scale neatly with an increasing number of participants. Subsequently, the data reduction demanded by the scalable VANET-based solutions may limit the usability of the application. Some of the data are filtered out or compressed to such a degree that they are no longer meaningful for the considered application.

The application discussed in this thesis, i.e., a cooperative traffic information system, aims at improving road safety and efficiency by reducing road congestion. Clearly such an application is highly desirable and urgently needed. We have therefore proposed a solution that allows implementing the application in an efficient way without the technological limitations imposed by the VANETs. Our first attempt to do so was PeerTIS: a peer-to-peer-based traffic information system built upon a mobile Internet access network (UMTS). Its design was based on the fact that TIS' participants will not request information about single street segments, but rather a set of consecutive segments forming a route to the planned destination will be requested. Typical peer-to-peer networks used for content sharing, however, destroy the interdependencies within the stored data by spreading the data randomly by means of consistent hashing all over the network. Thus the challenges we had to address are quite unique also in the peer-to-peer community. We show in Chapter 5 that the preservation of the structure of the data stored in the system yields a considerable performance improvement when compared to a generic content sharing peer-to-peer network. The first solution we proposed kept the street segments which form a route close together in the overlay structure by leaving hashing off and making the peers responsible for parts of the street map. Each peer is then responsible for all the measurements referring to its part of the map. Although such an adjusted peer-to-peer network already promised the feasibility of real-world implementations, it suffered from unfair load distribution. Some of the peers were responsible for parts of the map with no or only a few streets, thus contributing less resources. This undermines the philosophy of a cooperative traffic information system.

Therefore we departure even further from the classical DHTs and proposed GraphTIS in Chapter 6: a completely new peer-to-peer overlay algorithm which is based on the distributed storage of a routing graph. We have shown that this design tailored to the special needs of the considered application enables efficient storage and retrieval of traffic related data. A graph abstraction was used to describe the structure and the interdependencies of the data. The street segments forming possible routes were connected by edges in the graph. Each peer in our system was responsible for a small part of the original routing graph, i.e., a set of street segments and the corresponding traffic measurements. Our design aimed at keeping segments that are likely to be queried together in one subgraph. Furthermore, the peer-to-peer structure is built in such a way that the requests for a description of the traffic conditions along a route are passed from peer to peer as if they followed the route in the overlay. Such processing enable a quick retrieval of the relevant data, while the use of a graph instead of a map to distribute the data allows to avoid unfair load distribution. In fact, we achieved a load distribution comparable with that of a hash-based system, at the same time outperforming such a solution in terms of look-up performance.

After arriving at the point where requests for data could be realized efficiently and the data were fairly distributed among the participants, we addressed the last important function of a traffic information system. Since the stored data are dynamic (the traffic conditions change over time), a mechanism was required for keeping in touch with the development of the situation. A naive solution would be to request the data periodically, which however can lead to the wastage of resources. Thus we proposed a novel approach to distribute the updates in the cooperative traffic information system. Our solution utilizes a publish/subscribe paradigm. Instead of periodically requesting data, the participants publish their interests for a particular type of data (e.g., referring to their current route) in the form of subscriptions. As soon as the traffic conditions on a given route change significantly, all the subscribers are informed so that they can react accordingly by adjusting their routes. Our evaluation shows that such an approach can indeed significantly reduce the burden of keeping in touch with the development of the situation.

The technical feasibility and efficiency of the proposed solutions, as demonstrated in a realistic simulation study, marked an important step towards the practical usage of the discussed application. However, what was equally important, if not even more so, was to show that when applied the application can bring some real benefits to its potential users. Traffic information systems are meant to constitute a basis for dynamic routing of cars, allowing them to avoid traffic jams and find the fastest route to the planned destination. In this thesis we examined two distinct routing strategies that accounted for dynamic information about the traffic condition. Their evaluation in Chapter 7 used a full-fledged traffic simulator extended to facilitate the dynamic routing of the simulated cars. The presented results are quite optimistic: the majority of the simulated cars reached their destinations faster when dynamic routing and cooperative TIS were used. Subsequently, we identified an interesting interplay between the application and the user gains. For instance, by "optimizing" the traffic flow of the simulated cars we also further improved the load distribution in the peer-to-peer network: the traffic measurements were spread more homogeneously in the network (similarly to cars spread homogeneously over the alternative routes).

In summary, we have presented ways of implementing efficient cooperative traffic information systems. Our solution uses peer-to-peer overlays built upon infrastructure-based mobile Internet access networks. Most of the problems addressed in this thesis differ from the typical research questions discussed in the inter-vehicular and peer-to-peer communities. We strongly believe that the proposed algorithms may also be applied in other applications where structured data have to be stored and processed in an efficient, robust fashion. A quite obvious extension would be to store in the system not only information about driving conditions but also other data relevant to the drivers, such as information about parking lots, points of interest, etc. Such an extension would be quite easy to integrate, as it uses exactly the same addressing scheme. All the data relevant to the cars refer somehow to the street segments the cars are driving on, and our systems are built to efficiently store and distribute the data referring to street segments. Furthermore, a graph abstraction is widely used in computer science as many applications rely on it to store and process their data. Therefore it may be possible to use our solutions also outside the context of inter-vehicular applications.

Appendix

Appendix A

Lemma Proofs

A.1 Proof of Lemma 3.1

We first note that Δ is well-defined and positive because from $\delta r_0^2 > 1$ if follows that $\sqrt{\delta} - r_0^{-1} > 0$. We must show that for any circle C with radius $r \geq r_0$ less than δr^2 points can be fit into C, if the pair-wise distances between the points are all at least Δ. The latter is equivalent to stating that if we draw circles with radius $\frac{\Delta}{2}$ around each of the measurement points within C, then none of these small circles may intersect with each other.

Observe that the centers of all small circles must lie within C. Therefore, all the small circles are fully enclosed within a circle C^+ with the same center as C and radius $r + \frac{\Delta}{2}$. Thus, the total area of the small circles (each covering an area of $\pi(\Delta/2)^2$) is less than the area of C^+, which is $\pi(r + \Delta/2)^2$. (It is strictly less because C^+ can impossibly be fully covered by small circles.) Therefore, for the total number n of small circles (i.e., the total number of measurement points within C) it holds that

$$n < \frac{\pi(r + (\Delta/2))^2}{\pi(\Delta/2)^2} = \frac{r^2}{(\Delta/2)^2} + \frac{2r}{\Delta/2} + 1$$
$$= r^2 \left(\sqrt{\delta} - \frac{1}{r_0}\right)^2 + 2r\left(\sqrt{\delta} - \frac{1}{r_0}\right) + 1.$$

Because $r \geq r_0$, n is thus bounded above by

$$r^2 \left(\sqrt{\delta} - \frac{1}{r}\right)^2 + 2r\left(\sqrt{\delta} - \frac{1}{r}\right) + 1 = r^2 \delta.$$

Consequently, the max-density condition holds. □

A.2 Proof of Lemma 3.2

We show that when $\lfloor \frac{4r}{\Delta} \rfloor$ points are evenly distributed on the perimeter of a circle with radius $r \geq \frac{\Delta}{2}$, the distance between two neighboring points is at least Δ. The angle α between two neighboring such points on the circle is

$$\alpha = \frac{2\pi}{\lfloor \frac{4r}{\Delta} \rfloor} \geq \frac{2\pi}{\frac{4r}{\Delta}} = \frac{\pi}{2} \frac{\Delta}{r}.$$

The distance μ between the points is the base of an isosceles triangle with arm length r and angle α. Thus,

$$\mu = 2r \sin\left(\frac{\alpha}{2}\right).$$

Note that $\forall x \in [0, \pi/2]$ it holds that $\sin(x) \geq \frac{2x}{\pi}$, and also note that $\alpha < \pi$ (because $r \geq \frac{\Delta}{2}$ and thus $\lfloor \frac{4r}{\Delta} \rfloor \geq 2$). Therefore,

$$\mu \geq 2r \frac{2\alpha}{\pi} \geq 2r \frac{2}{\pi} \frac{\pi \Delta}{4r} = \Delta.$$

From the fact that the distance between each pair of neighboring points is at least Δ, it easily follows that all pair-wise distances are at least Δ. □

A.3 Proof of Lemma 3.3

First, we show a simple lemma which will be of great help.

Lemma A.1. *For all $k \in \mathbb{N}, k \geq 1$ and all $x \geq k$ it holds that*

$$\lfloor x \rfloor > \frac{k}{k+1} x.$$

Proof. For $x \in \mathbb{N}$ the assertion trivially holds. Thus, we focus on the case $x \notin \mathbb{N}$. Let $y := x - \lfloor x \rfloor$. Since $k \in \mathbb{N}$ and $x \geq k$ we also have $\lfloor x \rfloor \geq k$. Because $0 < y < 1$ we get

$$\frac{\lfloor x \rfloor}{y} > k \quad \Rightarrow \quad \lfloor x \rfloor > ky \quad \Rightarrow \quad \lfloor x \rfloor > k(x - \lfloor x \rfloor)$$
$$\Rightarrow \quad (k+1)\lfloor x \rfloor > kx \quad \Rightarrow \quad \lfloor x \rfloor > \frac{k}{k+1} x.$$

□

We now turn towards proving Lemma 3.3.

According to the definition of M^* above, the total number of measurement points in zone Z_i is

$$z_i = \sum_{j=0}^{w_i-1} \left\lfloor \frac{4(k_i - j\Delta)}{\Delta} \right\rfloor$$

Since $\frac{4(k_i - j\Delta)}{\Delta} > 1$ for any $j < w_i$, we can apply Lemma A.1 (with $k = 1$) and get

$$z_i > \sum_{j=0}^{w_i-1} \frac{2(k_i - j\Delta)}{\Delta}$$
$$= 2 \sum_{j=0}^{w_i-1} \frac{k_i}{\Delta} - 2 \sum_{j=0}^{w_i-1} j$$
$$= 2 \left\lfloor \frac{k_i - k_{i-1}}{\Delta} \right\rfloor \frac{k_i}{\Delta} - 2 \frac{(w_i - 1)w_i}{2}.$$

Since per definition $k_i > 8k_{i-1}$ and $\forall i \in \mathbb{N} : k_i \geq \Delta$ it holds that

$$\frac{k_i - k_{i-1}}{\Delta} > 7.$$

We may thus again apply Lemma A.1 (this time with $k = 7$) and obtain

$$z_i > \frac{7(k_i^2 - k_i k_{i-1})}{4\Delta^2} - (w_i - 1)w_i.$$

Recall that the number of circles in zone Z_i is

$$w_i = \left\lfloor \frac{k_i - k_{i-1}}{\Delta} \right\rfloor$$

and therefore

$$1 \leq w_i < \frac{k_i}{\Delta}.$$

Thus,

$$(w_i - 1)w_i < \frac{k_i^2}{\Delta^2}$$

and we arrive at

$$\begin{aligned} z_i &> \frac{7(k_i^2 - k_i k_{i-1})}{4\Delta^2} - \frac{k_i^2}{\Delta^2} \\ &= \frac{3}{4}\frac{k_i^2}{\Delta^2} - \frac{7}{4}\frac{k_i k_{i-1}}{\Delta^2} \\ &= \frac{1}{2}\frac{k_i^2}{\Delta^2} + \left(\frac{1}{4}\frac{k_i^2}{\Delta^2} - \frac{7}{4}\frac{k_i k_{i-1}}{\Delta^2}\right) \\ &= \frac{1}{2}\frac{k_i^2}{\Delta^2} + \left(\frac{(k_i - 7k_{i-1})k_i}{4\Delta^2}\right). \end{aligned}$$

Since per definition $k_i > 7k_{i-1}$, the term in parentheses is positive and thus

$$z_i > \frac{k_i^2}{2\Delta^2}.$$

This is the assertion. □

Appendix B

Range Queries

Among the subjects discussed in the peer-to-peer community, range queries are probably the closest to what is needed to implement a cooperative traffic information system in a distributed manner. Here we review the works on enabling range queries in P2P and show that they are not applicable in our specific setup of a traffic information system.

Classical DHTs use a hash function to determine which peer will be responsible for a given key. However, such hashing destroys the ordering of the keys and makes queries for all the keys within a given range hard to implement. Thus numerous extensions of DHTs or stand-alone P2P structures supporting range queries have been proposed [RM06].

The Multi-Addressable Network (MAAN) [CMCS03] is built upon Chord [SMLN+03] and uses a special form of "locality preserving" hashing to support range queries. The hashing keeps attributes with similar numerical values close together in the Chord ring. An example of such a hash function for an attribute with v values in range (v_{min}, v_{max}) would be:

$$H(v) = (v - v_{min}) \cdot (2^m - 1)/(v_{max} - v_{min})$$

If a peer wants to query for all values $l < v < u$ it uses the standard Chord routing to find the successor of l (the lower bound). Starting from the peer responsible for the beginning of the sought-after interval, the query travels along the Chord ring together with all the keys located from the interval. As soon as the query arrives at the successor of u, all the collected keys are sent back to the query originator. This approach is not directly applicable in a TIS application because we have to cope with data spread in a two-dimensional space, and Chord can handle only one-dimensional data either with or without the locality preserving hashing.

It would be possible to use two Chord rings: one mapping x coordinates of the keys and the other mapping y coordinates. Such a generalization was proposed in Mercury [BAS04], where multi-attribute range queries were addressed. The system consists of a number of Chord rings ("attribute hubs", as the authors call them) and each ring is searched independently. The authors did not use locality preserving hashing but rather left out hashing altogether. To answer a typical range query such as, finding all values for keys from:

$$\{(x,y) : x_1 < x < x_2, y_1 < y < y_2\}$$

Two rings have to be queried and all the keys from the given x and y interval range have to be located. The query originator receives both lists and merges them to find the keys fulfilling both criteria at the same time.

It should be noted that generally due to decentralization the query originator does not know which keys are currently used in the system. Thus all the keys from an interval have to be queried for. In the case of a TIS application, however, the participant knows exactly which keys are relevant (the segments of the planned route) and only those are included in a query.

Another way of extending existing DHTs to support range queries is to substitute hashing with space-filling curves (Hilbert curves, z-curves, etc.) to order the keys and to then map them onto a generic DHT. This approach was followed for instance in [AX02]. A Hilbert curve was also used to order the keys in a 2D Content Addressable Network (CAN) [RFH+01]. The CAN space is partitioned as usual (and the SFC as well), thus each peer is responsible for a part of the SFC (and the respective data). A range query is first sent (by means of greedy forwarding) to the peer responsible for the middle part of the interval. From this point on either "brute-force" flooding is initiated or "directed flooding" by passing the query to the direct neighbors. Since the SFC keeps the data with similar attribute values "close" in the peer-to-peer structure, such flooding has a limited range. Yet, again, this approach allows only for one-dimensional queries, which are not sufficient for an efficient realization of a TIS application.

A vast number of solutions for range queries in P2P networks are based on structures indexing multidimensional data, especially all kinds of tries. Again these indexes can be stored in a decentralized fashion in either existing and adjusted or completely new DHTs.

BATON (BAlanced Tree Overlay Network) [JOV05] is a distributed tree structure. Each tree node is maintained by a single peer. Both leaf and internal nodes are assigned a range of values. Each peer maintains links to its parent node, child nodes and the nodes at a distance of power of two at the same level in the tree. The BATON overlay structure behaves like an index tree (an AVL tree to be exact). For point queries a peer sends the query to the node from its routing table which is the rightmost node with an interval start smaller than the searched value (when the searched value is not in the same subtree as the originator). Alternatively, the search request is forwarded down the tree to the destination node whose range of index values contains the searched value. The range queries are handled as point queries but as soon as the peer responsible for a part of the interval is located the query is sent down in the tree structure to answer the query completely. [SOTZ07] extends this idea to support multidimensional queries. The authors used exactly the same algorithm to store and manage a K-D tree indexing a multidimensional key space. The queries are multidimensional "cubes" of attribute ranges. Such a structure could indeed store traffic information, if not efficiently. A query primitive used in this system is a minimal bounding box containing sought-after keys. The same holds true for other trie-based solutions such as [CLGS04] using P-Trees or DHR trees from [WS06]. In both cases the tries are stored in the ring structure of Chord.

It is important to point out that the minimal bounding box as a query primitive is

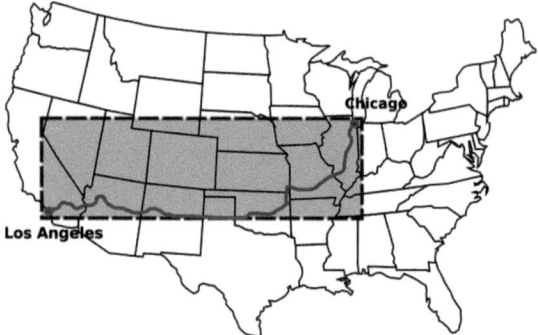

Figure B.1: Bounding box containing a planned journey (Route 66 from Chicago to Los Angeles).

not directly applicable to a traffic information system. To illustrate this, assume a traffic information system that is relying on a range query functionality as described above, i.e., on the ability to retrieve information from a given (n-dimensional) key interval. Assume that a driver wants to drive from Chicago to Los Angeles along Route 66. At the beginning of the journey he or she wants to be sure that the current traffic conditions are sufficiently good to enjoy the trip, and so produces a query for the traffic information system to retrieve all the relevant measurements:

$$(x, y) \in (x_{chicago}, x_{l.a}) \times (y_{chicago}, y_{l.a})$$

This would be the minimal bounding box containing Route 66 (Figure B.1). Clearly such a 2D interval includes a very large number of keys that are not relevant to the query—for instance routes heading in completely different directions.

A different approach to supporting range queries are systems which do not use DHTs but instead a skip lists or skip graphs [AS07]. A skip list is a distributed linked list containing all the keys maintained in the network. Each peer is responsible for a subinterval of the list. The peers are not only connected to direct neighbors (responsible for adjacent intervals) but also possess "shortcuts" to distant parts of the list. In order to locate a single key in the network a form of greedy forwarding towards the sought-after key is performed. Skip lists do not use hashing and thus are able to preserve the structure of the stored data and to naturally handle range queries. On the other hand, they are susceptible to load-balancing problems. An important observation is that a skip list can be (on a one-to-one basis) transformed into an unbounded random B-tree [AS07]. This feature allows for multidimensional range queries similar to those on the tries presented above. Consequently, they suffer from the same shortcomings of an insufficient query primitive.

Expressing a query for a sequence of segments forming a route as a sequence of independent point queries is clearly not efficient. On the other hand, querying for data within a bounding box results in the retrieval of irrelevant data. In this thesis we have present a new query primitive which suits the exact needs of a TIS application.

Bibliography

Own Publications

[GRSM09] Norbert Goebel, Jędrzej Rybicki, Björn Scheuermann, and Martin Mauve. A Peer-to-Peer-based Traffic Information System. In *MobiCom '09: Proceedings of the 15th ACM SIGMOBILE International Conference on Mobile Computing and Networking, Demo Track*, pages 10–11, September 2009. Technical Demonstration.

[KRM07] Wolfgang Kiess, Jędrzej Rybicki, and Martin Mauve. On the nature of Inter-Vehicle Communication. In *WMAN 07: Proceedings of the 4th Workshop on Mobile Ad-Hoc Networks*, pages 493–502, March 2007.

[LRSM08] Christian Lochert, Jędrzej Rybicki, Björn Scheuermann, and Martin Mauve. Scalable data dissemination for inter-vehicle-communication: Aggregation versus peer-to-peer. *Oldenbourg it – Information Technology*, 50(4):237–242, August 2008.

[RPSM11] Jędrzej Rybicki, Benjamin Pesch, Björn Scheuermann, and Martin Mauve. Supporting cooperative traffic information systems through street-graph-based peer-to-peer networks. In *KiVS '11: Proceedings of the GI/ITG Conference Communication in Distributed Systems*, pages 121–132, March 2011.

[RSK+07] Jędrzej Rybicki, Björn Scheuermann, Wolfgang Kiess, Christian Lochert, Pezhman Fallahi, and Martin Mauve. Challenge: Peers on wheels – a road to new traffic information systems. In *MobiCom '07: Proceedings of the 13th Annual ACM International Conference on Mobile Computing and Networking*, pages 215–221, September 2007.

[RSKM09] Jędrzej Rybicki, Björn Scheuermann, Markus Koegel, and Martin Mauve. PeerTIS - A Peer-to-Peer Traffic Information System. In

	VANET '09: Proceedings of the 6th ACM International Workshop on VehiculAr Inter-NETworking, pages 23–32, September 2009.
[RSM11]	Jędrzej Rybicki, Björn Scheuermann, and Martin Mauve. Peer-to-peer data structures for cooperative traffic information systems. *Elsevier Pervasive and Mobile Computing, Special Issue on Vehicular Sensor Networks and Mobile Sensing over Wide-Scale Deployment Environments*, 7(1), 2011.
[SLRM09]	Björn Scheuermann, Christian Lochert, Jędrzej Rybicki, and Martin Mauve. A fundamental scalability criterion for data aggregation in VANETs. In *MobiCom '09: Proceedings of the 15th Annual ACM International Conference on Mobile Computing and Networking*, pages 285–296, September 2009.

Other References

[3gp]	The 3rd Generation Partnership Project (3GPP). http://www.3gpp.org/.
[Ace]	The ACEA automobile industry pocket guide. http://www.acea.be/images/uploads/files/2010924_Pocket_Guide_2nd_edition.pdf.
[APR05]	Maen M. Artimy, William J. Phillips, and William Robertson. Connectivity with static transmission range in vehicular ad hoc networks. In *CNSR '05: Proceedings of the 3rd IEEE Annual Communication Networks and Services Research Conference*, pages 237–242, Washington, DC, USA, May 2005. IEEE Computer Society.
[AS07]	James Aspnes and Gauri Shah. Skip graphs. *ACM Transactions on Algorithms*, 3(4):37, 2007.
[ATS04]	Stephanos Androutsellis-Theotokis and Diomidis Spinellis. A survey of peer-to-peer content distribution technologies. *ACM Computing Surveys*, 36:335–371, 2004.
[AX02]	Artur Andrzejak and Zhichen Xu. Scalable, efficient range queries for grid information services. In *P2P '02: Proceedings of the 2nd IEEE International Conference on Peer-to-Peer Computing*, pages 33–42, August 2002.

[BAPI91]   Moshe Ben-Akiva, Andre De Palma, and Kaysi Isam. Dynamic network models and driver information systems. *Transportation Research Part A: General*, 25(5):251–266, 1991.

[BAS04]   Ashwin Bharambe, Mukesh Agrawal, and Srinivasan Seshan. Mercury: supporting scalable multi-attribute range queries. *ACM SIGCOMM Computer Communication Review*, 34(4):353–366, 2004.

[BCM04]   John W. Byers, Jeffrey Considine, and Michael Mitzenmacher. Geometric generalizations of the power of two choices. In *SPAA '04: Proceedings of the 16th ACM Symposium on Parallelism in Algorithms and Architectures*, pages 54–63, June 2004.

[BCTL08]   Nilanjan Banerjee, Mark D. Corner, Don Towsley, and Brian Neil Levine. Relays, base stations, and meshes: Enhancing mobile networks with infrastructure. In *MobiCom '08: Proceedings of the 14th Annual ACM International Conference on Mobile Computing and Networking*, pages 81–91, September 2008.

[BGL]   Boost Graph Library (BGL) . http://www.boost.org.

[BHK07]   Ingmar Baumgart, Bernhard Heep, and Stephan Krause. OverSim: A flexible overlay network simulation framework. In *Global Internet: Proceedings of 10th IEEE Global Internet Symposium*, pages 79–84, May 2007.

[BJ92]   Thang Nguyen Bui and Curt Jones. Finding good approximate vertex and edge partitions is NP-hard. *Elsevier Information Processing Letters*, 42(3):153–159, 1992.

[C2C]   Car–2–Car Communication Consortium. http://www.car–2–car.org/.

[CGM06]   Murat Caliskan, Daniel Graupner, and Martin Mauve. Decentralized discovery of free parking places. In *VANET '06: Proceedings of the 3rd ACM International Workshop on Vehicular Ad Hoc Networks*, pages 30–39, September 2006.

[CKF04]   Curt Cramer, Kendy Kutzner, and Thomas Fuhrmann. Bootstrapping locality-aware P2P networks. In *ICON '04: Proceedings of the IEEE International Conference on Networks*, pages 357–361, November 2004.

[CLGS04]   Adina Crainiceanu, Prakash Linga, Johannes Gehrke, and Jayavel Shanmugasundaram. Querying peer-to-peer networks using P-trees. In *WebDB '04: Proceedings of the 7th International Workshop on the Web and Databases*, pages 25–30, June 2004.

[CMCS03]   Min Cai, Frank Martin, Jinbo Chen, and Pedro Szekely. MAAN: A multi-attribute addressable network for grid information services. In *GRID '03: Proceedings of the 4th International Workshop on Grid Computing*, pages 184–192, November 2003.

[CMM95]   Eugene Inseok Chong, Sanjeev Maddila, and Steve Morley. On finding single-source single-destination k shortest paths. In *ICCI '95: Proceedings of 7th IEEE International Conference of Computing and Information*, pages 40 – 47. IEEE, July 1995.

[Coi99]   Benjamin Coifman. Using dual loop speed traps to identify detector errors. *Transportation Research Record*, 1683(1):47–58, 1999.

[CSS00]   Debashish Chowdhury, Ludger Santen, and Andreas Schadschneider. Statistical physics of vehicular traffic and some related systems. *Physics Reports*, 329(4–6):199 – 329, 2000.

[CWM94]   Gordon Cameron, Brian J. N. Wylie, and David McArthur. Paramics: moving vehicles on the connection machine. In *Proceedings of the ACM/IEEE Conference on Supercomputing*, pages 291–300, November 1994.

[DDS92]   Martin Desrochers, Jacques Desrosiers, and Marius Solomon. A new optimization algorithm for the vehicle routing problem with time windows. *Operations Research*, 40(2):342–354, 1992.

[DHJ+07]   Giuseppe DeCandia, Deniz Hastorun, Madan Jampani, Gunavardhan Kakulapati, Avinash Lakshman, Alex Pilchin, Swaminathan Sivasubramanian, Peter Vosshall, and Werner Vogels. Dynamo: Amazon's highly available key-value store. *SIGOPS Operating Systems Review*, 41(6):205–220, 2007.

[DJ07]   Sandor Dornbush and Anupam Joshi. StreetSmart Traffic: Discovering and disseminating automobile congestion using VANET's. In *VTC '07-Spring: Proceedings of the 65th IEEE Vehicular Technology Conference*, pages 11–15, April 2007.

[DKKS05]   Florian Doetzer, Florian Kohlmayer, Timo Kosch, and Markus Strassberger. Secure communication for intersection assistance. In *WIT '05: Proceedings of the 2nd International Workshop on Intelligent Transportation*, May 2005.

[dot05]   Traffic congestion and reliability: Trends and advanced strategies for congestion mitigation. Technical report, U.S. Department of Transportation, Federal Highway Administration, 1200 New Jersey Ave., SE, Washington, September 2005.

[DSR03] Standard specification for telecommunications and information exchange between roadside and vehicle system - 5 GHz band dedicated short range communications (DSRC) medium access control (MAC) and physical layer (PHY) specifications. Technical Report ASTM E2213-03, ASTM International, West Conshohocken, PA, September 2003.

[EFGK03] Patrick Th. Eugster, Pascal A. Felber, Rachid Guerraoui, and Anne-Marie Kermarrec. The many faces of publish/subscribe. *ACM Computer Surveys*, 35(2):114–131, 2003.

[EGH+06] Tamer ElBatt, Siddhartha Goel, Gavin Holland, Hariharan Krishnan, and Jayendra Parikh. Cooperative collision warning using dedicated short range wireless communications. In *VANET '06: Proceedings of the 3rd ACM International Workshop on Vehicular Ad Hoc Networks*, pages 1–9, September 2006.

[Enk03] Wilfried Enkelmann. FleetNet – Applications for Inter-Vehicle Communication. In *IV '03: Proceedings of the IEEE Intelligent Vehicles Symposium*, pages 162–167, June 2003.

[eSa] The eSafety support project. http://www.esafetysupport.org.

[FGS04] Bernhard Fleischmann, Stefan Gnutzmann, and Elke Sandvoss. Dynamic vehicle routing based on online traffic information. *Transportation Science*, 38(4):420–433, 2004.

[FKM+03] Holger Füßler, Michael Käsemann, Martin Mauve, Hannes Hartenstein, and Jörg Widmer. Contention-based forwarding for Mobile Ad-Hoc Networks. *Elsevier Ad Hoc Networks*, 1(4):351–369, 2003.

[Geo] The GeoNet project. http://www.geonet-project.eu.

[GG08] Chris GauthierDickey and Christian Grothoff. Bootstrapping of peer-to-peer networks. In *DaS-P2P '08: Proceedings of the 3rd International Workshop on Dependable and Sustainable Peer-to-Peer Systems*, pages 271 – 278, August 2008.

[GIO04] Samir Goel, Tomasz Imielinski, and Kaan Ozbay. Ascertaining viability of Wi-Fi based vehicle-to-vehicle network for traffic information dissemination. In *ITSC 04: Proceedings of the 7th International IEEE Conference on Intelligent Transportation Systems*, pages 1086–1091, October 2004.

[GK00] Piyush Gupta and P.R. Kumar. The capacity of wireless networks. *IEEE Transactions on Information Theory*, 46(2):388–404, 2000.

[GMT95]   John R. Gilbert, Gray L. Miller, and Shang-Hua Teng. Geometric mesh partitioning: implementation and experiments. In *IPPS '95: Proceedings of the 9th IEEE International Symposium on Parallel Processing*, pages 418–427, April 1995.

[gnu]   RFC-Gnutella. http://rfc-gnutella.sourceforge.net/.

[GT02]   Matthias Grossglauser and David N. C. Tse. Mobility increases the capacity of ad hoc wireless networks. *IEEE/ACM Transactions on Networking*, 10(4):477–486, 2002.

[HL95]   Bruce Hendrickson and Robert Leland. An improved spectral graph partitioning algorithm for mapping parallel computations. *SIAM Journal on Scientific Computing*, 16(2):452–469, 1995.

[IW08a]   Khaled Ibrahim and Michele C. Weigle. CASCADE: Cluster-based accurate syntactic compression of aggregated data in VANETs. In *GLOBECOM '08: Proceedings of the IEEE Global Telecommunications Conference – Workshops*, pages 1–10, November 2008.

[IW08b]   Khaled Ibrahim and Michele C. Weigle. Optimizing CASCADE data aggregation for VANETs. In *MoVeNet '08: Proceedings of the 2nd International Workshop on Mobile Vehicular Networks*, pages 724–729, September 2008.

[jab]   Jabber instant messaging system. http://www.jabber.org/.

[JOV05]   Hosagrahar V. Jagadish, Beng Chin Ooi, and Quang Hieu Vu. BATON: a balanced tree structure for peer-to-peer networks. In *VLDB '05: Proceedings of the 31st International Conference on Very Large Data Bases*, pages 661–672, September 2005.

[KBC+00]   John Kubiatowicz, David Bindel, Yan Chen, Steven Czerwinski, Patrick Eaton, Dennis Geels, Ramakrishna Gummadi, Sean Rhea, Hakim Weatherspoon, Westley Weimer, Chris Wells, and Ben Zhao. Oceanstore: An architecture for global-scale persistent storage. In *ASPLOS '00: Proceedings of the 9th International Conference on Architectural Support for Programming Languages and Operating Systems*, pages 190–201, November 2000.

[KHR07]   Alireza Keshavarz-Haddad and Rudolf Riedi. Bounds for the capacity of wireless multihop networks imposed by topology and demand. In *MobiHoc '07: Proceedings of the 8th ACM International Symposium on Mobile Ad Hoc Networking and Computing*, pages 256–265, September 2007.

[KHRR06] Alireza Keshavarz-Haddad, Vinay Ribeiro, and Rudolf Riedi. Broadcast capacity in multihop wireless networks. In *MobiCom '06: Proceedings of the 12th Annual ACM International Conference on Mobile Computing and Networking*, pages 239–250, September 2006.

[KHRW02] Daniel Krajzewicz, Georg Hertkorn, Christian Rössel, and Peter Wagner. SUMO (Simulation of Urban MObility): An open-source traffic simulation. In *MESM '02: Proceedings of the 4th Middle East Symposium on Simulation and Modelling*, pages 183–187, September 2002.

[KK98] George Karypis and Vipin Kumar. A fast and high quality multilevel scheme for partitioning irregular graphs. *SIAM Journal on Scientific Computing*, 20(1):359–392, 1998.

[KK03] Frans M. Kaashoek and David Karger. Koorde: a simple degree-optimal distributed hash table. In *IPTPS '03: Proceedings of the 2nd International Workshop on P2P Systems*, pages 20–21, February 2003.

[KL70] Brian W. Keringhan and Shen Lin. An efficient heuristic procedure for partitioning graphs. *The Bell System Technical Journal*, 49(1):291–308, February 1970.

[Kle00] Jon Kleinberg. The small-world phenomenon: an algorithm perspective. In *STOC '00: Proceedings of the 32nd Annual ACM Symposium on Theory of Computing*, pages 163–170, May 2000.

[KLL+97] David Karger, Eric Lehman, Tom Leighton, Rina Panigrahy, Matthew Levine, and Daniel Lewin. Consistent hashing and random trees: distributed caching protocols for relieving hot spots on the world wide web. In *STOC '97: Proceedings of the 29th annual ACM Symposium on Theory of Computing*, pages 654–663, May 1997.

[KOKM10] Markus Koegel, Thomas Ogilvie, Wolfgang Kiess, and Martin Mauve. Real-World Evaluation of C2X-Road Side Warning Devices. In *ISWPC '10: Proceedings of the IEEE International Symposium on Wireless Pervasive Computing*, pages 180–185, May 2010.

[KPDH08] Mohamed Kafsi, Panos Papadimitratos, Olivier Dousse, and Jean-Pierre Hubaux. VANET connectivity analysis. In *AutoNet '08: Proceedings of the 3rd IEEE Workshop on Automotive Networking and Applications*, December 2008.

[KSA02] Timo Kosch, Christian Schwingenschlögl, and Li Ai. Information dissemination in multihop inter-vehicle networks. In *ITSC '02: Proceedings of the 5th International IEEE Conference on Intelligent Transportation Systems*, pages 685–690, September 2002.

[LBH+06] Tim Leinmüller, Levente Buttyan, Jean-Pierre Hubaux, Frank Kargl, Rainer Kroh, Maxim Raya, and Elmar Schoch. SEVECOM: Secure vehicle communication. In *MobileSummit '06: 15th IST Mobile and Wireless Communication Summit*, pages 155–163, May 2006.

[LCC+02] Qin Lv, Pei Cao, Edith Cohen, Kai Li, and Scott Shenker. Search and replication in unstructured peer-to-peer networks. In *ICS '02: Proceedings of the 16th International Conference on Supercomputing*, pages 84–95, June 2002.

[lcl] Location code list. http://www.bast.de/nn_42544/DE/Aufgaben/-abteilung-f/referat-f4/Location-Code-List/location-code-list-start.-html.

[LCP+05] Eng Keong Lua, Jon Crowcroft, Marcelo Pias, Ravi Sharma, and Steven Lim. A survey and comparison of peer-to-peer overlay network schemes. *IEEE Communications Surveys and Tutorials*, 7(2):72–93, March 2005.

[LP02] Xiaozhou Li and C. Greg Plaxton. On name resolution in peer-to-peer networks. In *POMC '02: Proceedings of the 2nd ACM International Workshop on Principles of Mobile Computing*, pages 82–89, October 2002.

[LSCM07] Christian Lochert, Björn Scheuermann, Murat Caliskan, and Martin Mauve. The feasibility of information dissemination in vehicular ad-hoc networks. In *WONS '07: Proceedings of the 4th Annual Conference on Wireless On-demand Network Systems and Services*, pages 92–99, January 2007.

[LSL+08] Xu Li, Wei Shu, Minglu Li, Hong-Yu Huang, Pei-En Luo, and Min-You Wu. Performance evaluation of vehicle-based mobile sensor networks for traffic monitoring. *IEEE Transactions on Vehicular Technology*, 58(4):1647 – 1653, 2008.

[LSM07] Christian Lochert, Björn Scheuermann, and Martin Mauve. Probabilistic aggregation for data dissemination in VANETs. In *VANET '07: Proceedings of the 4th ACM International Workshop on Vehicular Ad Hoc Networks*, pages 1–8, September 2007.

[LSW+08] Christian Lochert, Björn Scheuermann, Christian Wewetzer, Andreas Luebke, and Martin Mauve. Data Aggregation and Roadside Unit Placement for a VANET Traffic Information System. In *VANET '08: Proceedings of the 5th ACM International Workshop on VehiculAr Inter-NETworking*, pages 58–65, September 2008.

[lte] 3GPP Release 8 — The LTE Release. http://www.3gpp.org/article/%-lte.

[MCC+09] Francisco Martinez, Juan-Carlos Cano, Carlos Calafate, Pietro Manzoni, and Jose Barrios. Assessing the feasibility of a VANET driver warning system. In *PM2HW2N '09: Proceedings of the 4th ACM Workshop on Performance Monitoring and Measurement of Heterogeneous Wireless and Wired Networks*, pages 39–45, October 2009.

[MNR02] Dahlia Malkhi, Moni Naor, and David Ratajczak. Viceroy: a scalable and dynamic emulation of the butterfly. In *PODC '02: Proceedings of the 21st Annual Symposium on Principles of Distributed Computing*, pages 183–192, July 2002.

[mou] 3G launched in Nepal. http://www.teliasonera.com/en/News-and-Archive/3G-launched-in-Nepal/.

[napa] Nap: Linux napster client. http://nap.sourceforge.net/.

[napb] Opennap: Open source napster server. http://opennap.sourceforge.net/.

[NDLI04a] Tamer Nadeem, Sasan Dashtinezhad, Chunyuan Liao, and Liviu Iftode. TrafficView: A scalable traffic monitoring system. In *MDM '04: Proceedings of the 5th IEEE International Conference on Mobile Data Management*, pages 13–26, January 2004.

[NDLI04b] Tamer Nadeem, Sasan Dashtinezhad, Chunyuan Liao, and Liviu Iftode. TrafficView: traffic data dissemination using car-to-car communication. *ACM SIGMOBILE Mobile Computing and Communications Review*, 8(3):6–19, July 2004.

[NEPN08] Mohammed Nekoui, Ali Eslami, and Hossein Pishro-Nik. Scaling laws for distance limited communications in vehicular ad hoc networks. In *ICC '08: Proceedings of the IEEE International Conference on Communications*, pages 2253–2257, May 2008.

[NNP+09]   Mohammad Nekoui, Daiheng Ni, Hossein Pishroik, Richa Prasad, Mohammad Kanjee, Hui Zhu, and Thai Nguyen. Development of a VII–enabled prototype intersection collision warning system. *International Journal of Internet Protocol Technology*, 4(3):173–181, 2009.

[NS92]   Kai Nagel and Michael Schreckenberg. A cellular automaton model for freeway traffic. *Journal de Physique I*, 2(115):2221–2229, 1992.

[NTCS99]   Sze-Yao Ni, Yu-Chee Tseng, Yuh-Shyan Chen, and Jang-Ping Sheu. The broadcast storm problem in a mobile ad hoc network. In *MobiCom '99: Proceedings of the 5th Annual ACM/IEEE International Conference on Mobile Computing and Networking*, pages 151–162, July 1999.

[NW03]   Moni Naor and Udi Wieder. Novel architectures for P2P applications: the continuous-discrete approach. In *SPAA '03: Proceedings of the 15th Annual ACM Symposium on Parallel Algorithms and Architectures*, pages 50–59, June 2003.

[OMN]   OMNeT++. http://www.omnetpp.org.

[OSM]   OpenStreetMap. http://www.openstreetmap.org.

[Pal07]   Claudio Enrico Palazzi. *Fast online gaming over wireless networks*. PhD thesis, University of California at Los Angeles, Los Angeles, CA, USA, 2007.

[PBB+08]   Dieter Pfoser, Sotiris Brakatsoulas, Petra Brosch, Martina Umlauft, Nektaria Tryfona, and Giorgos Tsironis. Dynamic travel time provision for road networks. In *GIS '08: Proceedings of the 16th ACM SIGSPATIAL International Conference on Advances in Geographic Information Systems*, pages 1–4, November 2008.

[PLO+06]   Joon-Sang Park, Uichin Lee, Soon Oh, Mario Gerla, and Desmond Lun. Emergency related video streaming in VANET using network coding. In *VANET '06: Proceedings of the 3rd ACM International Workshop on Vehicular Ad Hoc Networks*, pages 102–103, September 2006.

[PNGN07]   Hossein Pishro-Nik, Aura Ganz, and Daiheng Ni. The capacity of vehicular ad hoc networks. In *Allerton '07: Proceedings of the 45rd Annual Allerton Conference*, pages 1156–1163, September 2007.

[Pro99]   Simone Provvedi. Radio resource control (RRC) (protocol specification). Technical Report 25.331, 3GPP, 1999.

[PRR97]   C. Greg Plaxton, Rajmohan Rajaraman, and Andréa W. Richa. Accessing nearby copies of replicated objects in a distributed environment. In *SPAA '97: Proceedings of the 9th Annual ACM Symposium on Parallel Algorithms and Architectures*, pages 311–320, June 1997.

[PTSP07] Ramu Panayappan, Jayini Trivedi, Ahren Studer, and Adrian Perrig. VANET-based approach for parking space availability. In *VANET '07: Proceedings of the 4th ACM International Workshop on Vehicular Ad Hoc Networks*, pages 75–76, September 2007.

[PTV]   PTV AG. The VISSIM traffic simulator. http://www.ptvag.com/software/transportation-planning-traffic-engineering/software-system-solutions/vissim/.

[RCCL06] Charles L. Robinson, Lorenzo Caminiti, Derek Caveney, and Kenneth Laberteaux. Efficient coordination and transmission of data for cooperative vehicular safety applications. In *VANET '06: Proceedings of the 3rd ACM International Workshop on Vehicular Ad Hoc Networks*, pages 10–19, September 2006.

[RFH+01] Sylvia Ratnasamy, Paul Francis, Mark Handley, Richard Karp, and Scott Shenker. A scalable content-addressable network. In *SIGCOMM '01: Proceedings of the 2001 Conference on Applications, Technologies, Architectures, and Protocols for Computer Communications*, pages 161–172, August 2001.

[RM06]   John Risson and Tim Moors. Survey of research towards robust peer-to-peer networks: search methods. *Elsevier Computer Networks*, 50(17):3485–3521, 2006.

[Rot09]   Leon J. M. Rothkrantz. Dynamic routing using the network of car drivers. In *EATIS '09: Proceedings of the Euro American Conference on Telematics and Information Systems*, pages 1–8, June 2009.

[Ruh]   Ruhrpilot. http://www.ruhrpilot.de/.

[Sch03]   Jochen Schiller. *Mobile Communications*, pages 93–156. Pearson Education Limited, Edinburgh, second edition, 2003.

[seta]   SETI@home. http://setiathome.ssl.berkeley.edu/.

[Setb]   Habitat: United Nations Centre For Human Settlements. Global report on human settlements. http://www.unhabitat.org/downloads/docs/GRHS.1996.4.pdf.

[SHF08]   Mohsen Sardari, Faramarz Hendessi, and Faramarz Fekri. DMRC: dissemination of multimedia in vehicular networks using rateless codes. In *INFOCOM '08: Proceedings of the 27th Annual Joint Conference of the IEEE Computer and Communications Societies*, pages 182–187, April 2008.

[Sie]   Siemens mobility. http://www.mobility.siemens.com/.

[sim] sim^{TD}: Safe and intelligent mobility: Test field germany. http://-www.simtd.de.

[sky]   Skype. http://www.skype.com/.

[SLS07]   Srinivas Shakkottai, Xin Liu, and R. Srikant. The multicast capacity of large multihop wireless networks. In *MobiHoc '07: Proceedings of the 8th ACM International Symposium on Mobile Ad Hoc Networking and Computing*, pages 247–255, September 2007.

[SMLN+03]   Ion Stoica, Robert Morris, David Liben-Nowell, David Karger, M. Frans Kaashoek, Frank Dabek, and Hari Balakrishnan. Chord: a scalable peer-to-peer lookup protocol for Internet applications. *ACM/IEEE Transactions on Networking*, 11(1):17–32, 2003.

[SOTZ07]   Yanfeng Shu, Beng Chin Ooi, Kian-Lee Tan, and Aoying Zhou. Supporting multi-dimensional range queries in peer-to-peer systems. In *P2P '07: Proceedings of the 7th IEEE International Conference on Peer-to-Peer Computing*, pages 173–180, September 2007.

[SSC+10]   Christoph Sommer, Armin Schmidt, Yi Chen, Reinhard German, Wolfgang Koch, and Falko Dressler. On the feasibility of UMTS-based traffic information systems. *Elsevier Ad Hoc Networks*, 8(5):506–517, 2010.

[STBW02]   Ralf-Peter Schäfer, Kai-Uwe Thiessenhusen, Elmar Brockfeld, and Peter Wagner. A traffic information system by means of real-time floating-car data. In *ITS World Congress: Proceedings of the 9th World Congress on Intelligent Transportation Systems*, pages 211–214, October 2002.

[SXC06]   Haiying Shen, Cheng-Zhong Xu, and Guihai Chen. Cycloid: A constant-degree and lookup-efficient P2P overlay network. *Elsevier Performance Evaluation*, 63(3):195–216, 2006.

[TB10]   Ozan Tonguz and Mate Boban. Multiplayer games over Vehicular Ad-Hoc Networks: A new application. *Ad Hoc Networks, Special Issue on Vehicular Networks*, 8(5):531–543, 2010.

[tmc] Traffic message channel TMCProFM. http://www.t-traffic.de/.

[Tom] TomTom. HD Traffic. http://www.tomtom.com/hdtraffic.

[Tom05] TomTom. How TomTom HD Traffic^{TM} and IQ Routes^{TM} data provides the very best routing. Technical report, TomTom, 2005.

[Ton99] Dario Serafino Tonesi. UTRAN Iu interface radio access network application part (RANAP). Technical Report 25.413, 3GPP, 1999.

[U.S] U.S. Department of Transportation. ITS: Federal intelligent transportation systems. http://www.itsoverview.its.dot.gov.

[WBKS02] Joachim Wahle, Ana Lúcia C. Bazzan, Franziska Klügl, and Michael Schreckenberg. The impact of real-time information in a two-route scenario using agent-based simulation. *Transportation Research Part C: Emerging Technologies*, 10(5-6):399 – 417, 2002.

[WCML07] Christian Wewetzer, Murat Caliskan, Klaus Meier, and Andreas Luebke. Experimental Evaluation of UMTS and Wireless LAN for Inter-Vehicle Communication. In *ITST '07: Proceedings of the 7th International Conference on ITS Telecommunications*, pages 287–292, June 2007.

[WER+03] Lars Wischhof, André Ebner, Hermann Rohling, Matthias Lott, and Rüdiger Halfmann. SOTIS – a self-organizing traffic information system. In *VTC '03-Spring: Proceedings of the 57th IEEE Vehicular Technology Conference*, pages 2442–2446, April 2003.

[WPR+08] Axel Wegener, Michal Piorkowski, Maxim Raxa, Horst Hellbrück, Stefan Fischer, and Jean-Pierre Hubeaux. TraCI: An interface for coupling road traffic and network simulators. In *CNS '08: Proceedings of the 11th Communications and Networking Simulation Symposium*, pages 155–163, April 2008.

[WS98] Duncan J. Watts and Steven H. Strogatz. Collective dynamics of "small-world" networks. *Nature*, 393(4):409–410, 1998.

[WS06] Xinfa Wei and Kaoru Sezaki. DHR-trees: A distributed multi-dimensional indexing structure for P2P systems. In *ISPDC '06: Proceedings of the 5th International Symposium on Parallel and Distributed Computing*, pages 281–290, July 2006.

[WSA02] Bernhard H. Walke, Peter Seidenberg, and Marc P. Althoff. *UMTS: The Fundamentals*. John Wiley Limited, Chichester, first edition, 2002.

[WSGLA08] Zheng Wang, Hamid R. Sadjadpour, and J. J. Garcia-Luna-Aceves. A unifying perspective on the capacity of wireless ad hoc networks. In *INFOCOM '08: Proceedings of the 27th Annual Joint Conference of the IEEE Computer and Communications Societies*, pages 753–762, April 2008.

[XB06] Huaying Xu and Matthew Barth. An adaptive dissemination mechanism for intervehicle communication-based decentralized traffic information systems. In *ITSC '06: Proceedings of the 9th International IEEE Conference on Intelligent Transportation Systems*, pages 1207–1213, September 2006.

[XK04] Liang-Liang Xie and P. R. Kumar. A network information theory for wireless communication: Scaling laws and optimal operation. *IEEE Transactions on Information Theory*, 50(5):748–767, May 2004.

[XMKS04] Qing Xu, Tony Mak, Jeff Ko, and Raja Sengupta. Vehicle-to-vehicle safety messaging in DSRC. In *VANET '04: Proceedings of the 1st ACM International Workshop on Vehicular Ad Hoc Networks*, pages 19–28, October 2004.

[YC05] Hsu-Hao Yang and Yen-Liang Chen. Finding k shortest looping paths in a traffic-light network. *Computers & Operations Research*, 32(3):571–581, 2005.

[YGM02] Beverly Yang and Hector Garcia-Molina. Improving search in peer to peer networks. In *ICDCS '02: Proceedings of the 22nd International Conference on Distributed Computing Systems*, pages 5–11, July 2002.

[YLE04] Chai-Kiat Yeo, Bu-Sung Lee, and Meng Hwa Er. A survey of application level multicast techniques. *ACM SIGCOMM Computer Communications Review*, 27(15):1547–1568, 2004.

[YLSW10] Yang Yang, Xu Li, Wei Shu, and Min-You Wu. Quality evaluation of vehicle navigation with CPS. In *GLOBECOM '10: Proceedings of the IEEE Global Communications Conference*, December 2010. To appear.

[ZJX07] Qi Zhao, Liu Jiaoyao, and Jingdong Xu. Improving search on Gnutella-like P2P systems. In *ICCS '07: Proceedings of the 7th International Conference on Computational Science*, pages 877–880, May 2007.

Index

Symbols

P-tree 167
sim^{TD} 26
"need to say" principle 16
2G 56
3G .... 55 f
3GPP 56

A

ad-hoc networks 24
addressing schema 21
AES 58
aggregation .... 13, 37, 44 f, 54
    aggregation level 37
    aggregation ratio 14
air interface .... 57 f
asymptotic scalability ... 38, 68, 116
attribute hubs 166
authentication key 58
authentication token 58
average flow speed 18, 138
AVL tree 167

B

backbone network 31
bandwidth profile 38
    example 45
base station 36, 58
BATON 167
beacon frequency 20, 52
beaconing 20

BFS 118
BMBF 25
BMVBS 10
BMWi 26
bootstrapping 69, 114
Bosch 25
broadcast .... 13, 28, 59 f, 70, 140
    broadcast storm 19
    medium 16, 20
    period 14
brute-force detection 69

C

C2CCC 25, 28
C2X 30
CAN 68, 77, 86, 90, 95, 166
capacity . 2, 13, 23, 37, 42, 44, 61, 73
capacity scaling laws 37
car clusters 34
car movement pattern 34, 41
car sensors 28
Car-to-X .... see C2X
car-to-x communication .... see C2X
CASCADE 135
CCW 28
cell phone .... see mobile station
cellular networks 17, 36, 73
CFPD 11
Chord 66, 80, 90, 95, 117, 165
communication paradigm 19, 37, 139
connectivity graph 35
Consistent Hashing 65

185

Content Addressable Network ... *see* CAN
content publishing 20
contention-based forwarding 25
cooperative TIS .. 21, 25, 61, 74, 92, 117, 137, 165
cost function 18
cost-benefits analysis 36
critical car density 35
critical phase connectivity 34
cross traffic 29
current traffic state 21

D

data filtering 16
data rate 40
data validation 14
de Bruijn Graph 68
deployment strategies 25
DHR-tree 167
DHT ... 77, 82, 88, 90, 119, 133, 165
diffusion .... *see* dissemination
digital street map 21
Dijkstra's Algorithm ... 84, 108, 118, 141, 143
dissemination 13, 16, 38, 41, 135
Distance Halving 68
distance-weighed throughput metric 37
Distributed Hash Table ... *see* DHT
DNS 69
DSL 59
DSRC 24, 30
DTN 35, 39
dynamic routing 21, 54, 79, 84, 133 f, 144
    AltRoute 142
    greedy algorithm 141

E

ECL 10

EEBL 28
end-to-end connectivity 35
eSafety 26
Ethernet 70
explicit retrieval 20

F

FCD 11, 134
FCW 28
finger table 67
FleetNet 25
Flexible Message Dispatcher 29
Floating Car Data .... *see* FCD
flooding 19, 30
frequency band 57
frequency spectrum 24

G

geographical routing 25
Geojoins 82, 115
GeoNet 26
GM 118
Gnutella 63
gossiping 39
GPS 13, 18, 21, 29, 74
Graph partitioning 102
    Geometric partitioning 103
    Graph growing partitioning . 103
    Kernighan-Lin Algorithm ... 103
    Spectral partitioning 103
GraphTIS 96, 112, 133
greedy forwarding 166
GSM 9, 11, 56, 86

H

highway scenario 13, 35, 134
Hilbert curve 166
historical traffic measurements 8
hot spot 82
HSDPA 59, 91
HSUPA 59, 91

I

inductive loops 9
infinite buffer sizes 44
information flow 44
infrastructure-based networks 17, 61, 73
initial routing decision 35
intelligent infrastructure 29
    intelligent parking automats . 31
    intelligent parking lots 31
    intelligent warning triangles .. 30
Intelligent Transportation System 7, 24
Intelligent Vehicle Safety Systems 26
interconnected base stations *see* RSU
IP-based communication 17, 58 – 61
ISO 24
ITS 24
IVC 1, 23, 32
    research projects 27

K

K-D tree 167
key neighbor graph 100, 119
key space ... 65, 77, 81, 95 f, 99, 125, 167
Kleinberg graph 111
knowledge base 13, 51
Koorde 68

L

LAN 70
landmarks 16, 45
latency 31, 33
LCA 28
LCL 10
limited bandwidth 33
limited connectivity 34
local authentication 58
locality preserving hashing 165
locality properties 75
long range link 111
look-up 65, 75, 86, 98, 119
look-up complexity
    CAN 68
    Chord 66, 90
    GraphTIS 110
    Koorde 68
    PeerTIS 80
lossy compression 15
LTE 59

M

MAAN 165
Manhattan metric 111
massive multi-player games 33
max-density condition 40, 49
maximum bandwidth 42
MD5 100
measurement point 40, 47
Mercury 166
MIMO 44
minimal bounding box 167
mixed reality multi-player games . 33
mobile Internet access 33, 55
mobile networks 36
mobile station 17, 58, 75
mobile traffic sensors 12
mulit-attribute range queries 166
multi-hop communication 24, 31
multicast 17, 37, 140
multidimensional cubes 167
multidimensional indexing structures 167
multiplexing
    frequency division multiplex .. 57
    time division multiplex 57
mutal authentication 58

N

Nagel-Schreckenberg model 138

navigation system.... *see* navigation unit
navigation unit... 10, 22, 35, 73, 86, 123, 133
NEC............................25
network load....................17
network operator.........11, 17, 58
network partition................55
NP-hard........................103

O

OpenStreetMap........79, 101, 143
optimal traffic flow...............18
overlap graphs..................104
overreaction....................137
oversaturation..................137

P

P2P...............*see* peer-to-peer
partitioning tree...........105, 118
peer-to-peer..61, 64, 73, 84, 95, 165
PeerTIS......................73, 80
penetration ratio 25, 35, 86, 128, 136
physical layer....................24
PITA............................12
Plaxton routing..................64
point of interest.................32
point query....................167
primary circle...................48
protocol standards...............24
Publish/Subscribe..........20, 140

R

range queries..................165
rebroadcast.....................30
relays...........................36
request/reply paradigm..........20
road safety applications.. *see* Safety applications
road segment.... *see* street segment
Route 66......................167

route adaptation.................22
routing table.......63, 77, 121, 167
RSU..................12, 16, 31, 33
RuhrPilot........................9

S

Safety applications
  After-crash Warning System.30
  Cooperative Collision Warning Systems..................28
  Curve Speed Warning........29
  Electronic Emergency Brake Light.....................28
  Emergency Brake Light......28
  Emergency Brake Warning...29
  Forward Collision Warning...28
  Intelligent Warning Triangles.30
  Intersection Assistance.......29
  Intersection Violation Warning 29
  Lane Change Assistance.....28
  Stop Sign Assistance.........29
  Traffic Signal Violation......29
sampling rate...................12
scalable dissemination..........50
secondary circle.................48
secure incentives................33
self-scalability..............86, 128
sending power..... *see* transmission power
Sevecom.......................26
SFC...........................166
SHA-1..........................66
skip graphs....................168
skip list........................168
Small-world graph..............113
SOTIS..............13, 18, 51, 134
spacial medium reuse............42
static wireless multi-hop networks 38
stationary traffic sensors.......9, 20
stop-and-go traffic...............7

store-and-forward principle ... 13, 17
street network's utilization 18
street segment 21, 40, 74, 84, 96, 143, 147
StreetSmart 16
structured peer-to-peer networks 64, 77
subscription broker 140
super-critical phase connectivity . 34
supporting infrastructure 35

T

temporary identities 58
TIS 1, 8, 12, 73, 75, 133
TMC 9f
TomTom HD Traffic 11, 60
total edge cut 102
traffic "congestion" 7
traffic congestion 2
traffic density 22
Traffic Efficiency Applications 31
    Parking lots guidance 31
    Traffic Information Systems . see TIS
Traffic Eye 9
traffic flow 10
traffic jam 21
traffic measurements . 13, 18, 21f, 35
traffic simulator 79
    Paramics 135
    setdes 135
    SUMO 79, 84, 118, 136
    VISSIM 136
TrafficView 14, 135
transmission power 24
travel time ... 18, 21, 45, 74, 84, 133, 143
trie 167
TTL 63

U

U. S. Department of Transportation 7

UE .... see mobile station
UMTS 17, 55f, 73, 86
    architecture 56
    cell 11, 17, 60, 86
    cell capacity 60, 88
    CN 56
    data rate 59
    Dedicated Channels 17
    EIR 57
    Fast Traffic Alter Protocol ... 17
    Forward Access Channel 17
    GGSN 57
    HLR 57
    IMSI 58
    Location Area Index 59
    location management 59
    MILENAGE 58
    MSC 57
    Multimedia Broadcast Multicast Service 17
    Node B 56
    PDP context 58
    PUK 58
    Random Access Channel 17
    RNC 56, 58
    RNS 56
    SGSN 57f
    SIM 58
    UTRA-FDD 57
    UTRA-TDD 57
    UTRAN 56
    VLR 57
unexpected traffic 16
unicast communication 37
unstructured peer-to-peer networks 63
update frequency 20, 37

V

Value-added applications 32
    Ad distribution 33

Games 33
Infotainment 32
VANET 1, 24, 73
    field tests 26
    market introduction 32, 54
    roll-out phase 16, 34
VANET scalability 37
vehicle-highway systems 24
Vehicular Ad-Hoc Networks ..... *see* VANET
Viceroy 68
VRP 138

W

W-CDMA 57
WiMax 55
wireless meshes 36
wireless network model 39
WLAN 24

X

XML 17

Z

z-curve 166

Die VDM Verlagsservicegesellschaft sucht für wissenschaftliche Verlage abgeschlossene und herausragende

Dissertationen, Habilitationen, Diplomarbeiten, Master Theses, Magisterarbeiten usw.

für die kostenlose Publikation als Fachbuch.

Sie verfügen über eine Arbeit, die hohen inhaltlichen und formalen Ansprüchen genügt, und haben Interesse an einer honorarvergüteten Publikation?

Dann senden Sie bitte erste Informationen über sich und Ihre Arbeit per Email an *info@vdm-vsg.de*.

Sie erhalten kurzfristig unser Feedback!

VDM Verlagsservicegesellschaft mbH
Dudweiler Landstr. 99   Telefon +49 681 3720 174
D - 66123 Saarbrücken   Fax   +49 681 3720 1749
www.vdm-vsg.de

Die VDM Verlagsservicegesellschaft mbH vertritt

Printed by Books on Demand GmbH, Norderstedt / Germany